BIG THINKERS
and BIG IDEAS

BIG THINKERS and BIG IDEAS

An INTRODUCTION to EASTERN and WESTERN PHILOSOPHY FOR KIDS

SHARON KAYE, PhD

ROCKRIDGE PRESS

Interior and Cover Designer: Jane Archer
Art Producer: Michael Hardgrove
Editor: Barbara Isenberg
Production Editor: Jenna Dutton

Illustration © 2020 Tara Sunil Thomas, cover, pp. 28, 46, 54, 61, 73, 80, 84, 99, 100, 130, 137.

Interior art used under license from © Shutterstock.com & iStockphoto.com.

Author photo courtesy of © Sally Al-Qaraghuli

ISBN: Print 978-1-64739-103-4 | eBook 978-1-64739-104-1
R0

For Tris, Audrey, and Xavier,
with all my love

CONTENTS

INTRODUCTION

What if I told you I see colors differently from you? For example, I see grass as red, which you see as green. Clouds, which you see as white, I see as black. Since my sight was this way from birth, I describe the colors of these things the same way you do. So, I call red "green," black "white," and so on.

How would you ever prove I was seeing the world wrong? Since you can't get inside my head and I can't get inside yours, we can't compare.

Suppose it turned out that half of the world sees colors like I do, while the other half sees them like you. Now who's right and who's wrong?

What if this situation is really true? How do we know people actually see colors—or anything else for that matter—the same way?

Is there any right or wrong when it comes to how we see the world?

Have you ever thought about deep questions like these? This is what philosophy is all about. Philosophy is both fun and good for your brain. By thinking about deep questions, anyone, including you, can be a philosopher.

WHAT IS PHILOSOPHY?

So, you think you'd like to be a philosopher, but don't know where to begin? You are in luck! The book you are holding in your hands is a great place to start. It is full of popular philosophical questions and activities to exercise your mind and encourage deep thinking. It's always best to start at the beginning, so we'll start there. What is philosophy, anyway?

Origins of Philosophy

The word "philosophy" comes from the Greek words for "love of wisdom." The term was coined by Socrates, a humble sculptor who lived in ancient Athens. Athens was the world's first **democracy**—it had a government run by the people.

Socrates was proud of his fellow Athenians for building such an advanced society. But he still had many questions about whether or not their society was good. He felt that a good society would be based on deep truths about **reality**, knowledge, **logic**, and justice.

Socrates asked his fellow Athenians to think about these deep truths. They became angry because they had no clear answers. They worried young people would think they were stupid and would begin to doubt their authority. They arrested Socrates and charged him with impiety (sinfulness) and corrupting, or spoiling, the youth.

Even at his trial, Socrates refused to stop asking deep questions. He believed that searching for the truth is important to improve society and save it from self-destruction. Sadly, the jury found Socrates guilty and he was put to death with poison hemlock.

Although the question-haters won that battle, they lost the war. The youth who admired Socrates were so angered by his death that they set up a school called the Academy in his honor. It became the world's first university—a place where people could gather to study any questions they wanted to.

It's been more than 2,400 years since Socrates's death. Today, universities in the world number in the tens of thousands! Do you think Socrates was right? Has searching for the truth improved society and saved it from self-destruction?

Discussion and Debate

How do people learn at universities?

They learn by discussing ideas. This is the method Socrates taught. He showed us that the truth doesn't grow on trees like apples. You can't just pick a truth or thought and consider it fact. It's not so simple. Every fact is just one way of seeing things. You must look at every fact in different ways to decide what is true. You can do this by discussing them.

For example, I was taught in third grade that Christopher Columbus discovered America. I thought this was a fact. But there were already people in America when Christopher Columbus arrived—the Native Americans. So did he really discover it? What do you think the Native Americans would have to say about that? It's important to consider how the arrival of European settlers looked from the Native Americans' point of view.

I wish I had the chance to discuss this question with my class in third grade. But when I was growing up, kids weren't encouraged to be philosophers. Teachers worried that if they let kids question what they were teaching, chaos would break loose.

Thankfully, this is changing.

Kids make excellent philosophers. Why? Kids are naturally curious about everything. True, discussion takes longer than just memorizing whatever your teacher says, but the time is well spent. Every time you think about what you are learning, you get closer to the truth.

In Socrates's day, most people believed the Earth was flat. They also thought there was nothing wrong with slavery. Look how far we have come! But we aren't finished yet. What beliefs do we have today that will make future people cringe?

There is only one way to find out. We need to keep on questioning and discussing.

For philosophers, discussions often turn into **debate**. This is the second way we learn. A debate is a respectful disagreement. Each side of the disagreement listens to and tries to disprove the opposite view.

I may not agree with your viewpoint, but this doesn't mean we are enemies. Just the opposite—philosophers are thankful for their opponents! In martial arts, we bow to each other, grateful for a challenge that will help us improve ourselves. It's the same with a debate. My reasons may change your mind, or your reasons may change my mind, or we may continue to disagree. One thing is for sure—debate improves our understanding and increases wisdom.

Branches of Philosophy

Although Socrates coined the term "philosophy," he was not the first philosopher. People all around the world have been asking deep questions, discussing, and debating since the beginning of human history. But Socrates' university system made philosophy into a subject for study. There are four main concepts in philosophy. They are **metaphysics**, **epistemology**, **ethics**, and **logic**. Let's look at each.

METAPHYSICS | REALITY

The study of reality is called metaphysics, from the Greek words *meta ta physika*, meaning "beyond physics." Physics is a science that studies matter and motion—things we can see and touch. In physics you might measure how much time it takes a marble to roll down a slide. But in metaphysics, we ask questions about what it means to exist. What is time? What is motion? Who are you? Are you one single thing or a number of things? What are numbers? Why is there a world at all? Where did it come from?

EPISTEMOLOGY | KNOWLEDGE

The study of knowledge is called epistemology, from the Greek word *episteme*, meaning "knowledge." If you were studying epistemology, these are some of the questions you might ask: Where does knowledge come from? How do we know the things we think we know? What is the difference between fact and opinion? Can we be certain of anything? Are my feelings reliable? Is doubting good or bad? Does **faith** count as a way of knowing? Can something be true for one person but not for someone else?

ETHICS | VALUES

The study of **moral** values, or what is right and wrong, is called ethics. Remember that all of Socrates's deep questions were inspired by his concern to make Athens a good society. What is a good life for human beings? How can we find happiness? Is it okay to be selfish sometimes or is selfishness always wrong? What about lying? What about violence? Should we judge our actions by the purposes behind them or by their results? Which is more important, family or friends?

 # LOGIC | CRITICAL THINKING

The study of good reasoning is called logic. Logic is what people use to figure out if something is true or false. When philosophers debate an issue, they make an argument for their side. Logic makes us ask questions like the following: How do you build an argument? Are there different kinds of arguments? What is the difference between a good argument and a bad argument? How is an argument like a math equation? Are any arguments unquestionable? What are the most common mistakes people make when arguing?

Why study philosophy?

Your head may be swimming with all these questions. Don't worry! You don't have to think about them all in one day, one month, or even one year. Philosophy is something you can study your whole life. I've been studying philosophy for thirty years now, and I still have a lot more to learn. Once you get started and see how the love of wisdom can improve your day-to-day experience, it will become part of you. Then, you'll always see things through a philosopher's eyes. I'll give you one small example.

I love my dog, Wizard, and I treat him very well. One day, how-ever, I wanted to take him for a long walk. Wizard didn't want to go, probably because he sensed it was going to rain. I made him go. We got soaked.

I thought getting caught in a downpour was kind of fun, but Wizard was angry and wouldn't sit by me that evening like he usually does. My son said I should tell him, "I'm sorry." I laughed and said that Wizard is just a dog. My son objected, "Dogs are people, too!"

That argument stopped me in my tracks. I thought long and hard about it. Then I read about some philosophers who see "human" and "person" as two separate categories that can apply to different things. In the end, I decided my son was right. Wizard wasn't a "human," but he was a "person."

Seeing Wizard as a nonhuman person has boosted our relation-ship in so many ways. Most of my friends still say Wizard is just a dog, and they say I'm a little bit crazy. But people said Socrates was crazy, too, so I figure I'm in good company.

Questions about Reality:

WHAT IS REAL?

Did you ever have an imaginary friend? Or did you ever play an imagination game that was so much fun it seemed more real than your real life? Maybe you built a fort or pretended to be royalty in a castle. Perhaps you had a pet monster living under your bed.

As you grew up, people probably told you that the ideas in your head weren't real. But philosophers aren't so sure about that. In fact, philosophers often wonder why most people assume that the world we see around us is the only one that is real. Is it?

Does anything EXIST?

oes anything exist?

"Of course!" you may say, pointing to the world outside your window. *"Lots of things! A tree, a city, a whole world . . ."*

But wait. What if I told you that you are a character I created for a virtual reality video game? You've written stories at school about fictional people in imaginary worlds, right? Well, pretend I'm an alien with advanced technology. I created "you" and "your world." Everything you have ever experienced in life is pure fiction, just part of a video game I made up.

"Impossible!" you would probably answer.

Why? My claim that your reality is fiction may seem unlikely, but it's hard to prove false. Taking this possibility seriously is a useful **thought experiment**. It has led philosophers throughout history to many conclusions about what, if anything, actually exists.

ADI SHANKARACHARYA was an eighth-century Indian philosopher who believed that the whole world is an illusion, or fantasy. According to Shankaracharya, what we see around us comes from the highest reality, Brahman. While Brahman is never-ending and unchanging, everything it makes is temporary and unreal. We ourselves are real only because we have Brahman within us.

The eighteenth-century Irish philosopher **GEORGE BERKELEY** claimed that thought is the only true reality. He thought of God as a giant mind. Rather than making a physical world—one that we can see and touch—God simply makes other minds and sends physical feelings to them. Berkeley felt that the idea of physical reality doesn't make any sense.

For the twentieth-century Russian philosopher **AYN RAND**, the existence of the physical world is an axiom. By this, she means its existence is obvious. It doesn't need to be proved. We should start with the objects we see around us and build our ideas of reality from there.

PLATO was an ancient Greek philosopher who noticed a big difference between our minds and the physical world. In our minds, we can think of perfect things, but in the world, nothing perfect exists. For example, imagine two sticks that are equal to each other in every way. Could you ever find such equality in the world? No. So then where does your idea of equality come from? It must come from someplace else—a perfect place that you visit only through thought. Plato called this place the World of Forms and argued that the physical world is nothing but a shadow of it.

PAUL *and* **PATRICIA CHURCHLAND** are present-day American philosophers who support the opposite view, that *only* the physical world exists. They argue that ideas are just energy flowing through nerves in our brains. You might say you can picture two perfectly equal sticks in your mind, but this is just an incorrect way of explaining. In reality, there is no picture, no equality, and no mind for them to exist in. What you are trying to describe is better explained using the language of science. A brain scanner can measure your thought as a physical reaction just like any other physical reaction in the world.

THINK ON IT!

How would you prove you're not a character in a virtual reality video game? Remember, this game is based on technology beyond anything you have seen. It can create a cupcake that feels moist and soft, smells sweet, and tastes great—simply by sending you electronic messages. How would you tell the difference between a virtual cupcake and a physical cupcake? If there is no way to tell them apart, are they equally real?

Why is there SOMETHING rather than NOTHING?

**W**e may not know exactly what is out there in the universe. But let's say there is something. The question is, why? Why isn't there nothing at all? Take a moment to imagine that nothing exists. Can you picture nothingness? What would it look like? If it looked like anything at all, then it wouldn't be nothing, would it?

When you are thinking about nothing, are you thinking about something? If you're not thinking about anything, then you can't be thinking about nothing. But if you're thinking about something, then it isn't nothing! Yikes! The very idea of nothing quickly becomes a philosophical puzzle.

The seventeenth-century Dutch philosopher **BARUCH SPINOZA** stated that it is impossible for there to be nothing. His reason is that the universe is necessary. Everything that exists has to exist exactly the way it does and everything that happens has to happen that way. There just is no room for anything to be otherwise.

Present-day Canadian theoretical physicist **LAWRENCE M. KRAUSS**, however, takes the opposite view. Scientists define things that exist in terms of their positive energy. But they have recently discovered great quantities of negative energy that balance out the positive energy, so that the total energy of the universe is zero. In this unstable nothingness, particles can unexpectedly pop into existence.

ZHOU DUNYI was an eleventh-century Chinese philosopher who thought that the many things we see around us came from the Great Ultimate. The Great Ultimate was unformed, but was not nothing. Through rest and movement, the everlasting laws of *yin* and *yang* created *qi*. *Qi* is the life force and physical energy of the universe.

According to seventeenth-century German philosopher **G.W. LEIBNIZ**, the only way to explain why there is something rather than nothing is God. Leibniz supported the Principle of Sufficient Reason, which says that there is a reason for everything that exists. The universe exists, so there must be a reason for it. But that reason has to be very special. It has to be something that does not need something else to explain it. It has to be self-explanatory—something that explains itself. Only God is self-explanatory because he is the only necessary being. The universe must exist because God wanted it to.

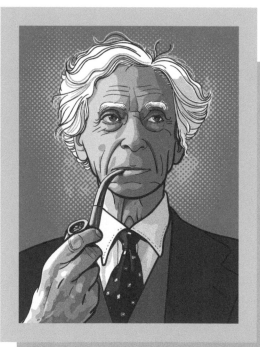

Twentieth-century English philosopher **BERTRAND RUSSELL** argued that the universe doesn't need a reason to exist. He agreed with the Principle of Sufficient Reason in that everything we experience can be explained. However, he pointed out that we don't ever experience the universe. We only experience small pieces of it—a sneeze, a rainstorm, a shooting star. Each of those things can be explained. But is there an explanation for the whole universe? No. The whole is a "brute fact." It just *is*. Russell rejected the idea of a necessary being and did not believe in the existence of God.

THINK ON IT!

The idea of nothingness is mind-boggling. But before you give up on it, think of yourself. Weren't you once nothing? Think of a moment a long time ago—maybe when the dinosaurs walked the Earth. What were you then? Were you something or nothing? If you were nothing, when exactly did you become something? If you were always something, what (and where) were you?

Where did the UNIVERSE come from?

Throughout history, people all around the world have looked up at the starry sky and wondered where this big, beautiful universe could have come from. For many people, like Leibniz (page 16), the question leads to a supreme being like God. For others, like Krauss and Russell (pages 16 and 15), it leads to nothing. Still other philosophers insist that the universe didn't come from anywhere, because it has always existed.

"Impossible!" you might think.

But why? Those who believe in God also believe God is **eternal**. This means God has always existed. If God has no beginning, then why can't the universe have no beginning?

According to the **KUBA** people of Central Africa, a white giant called Mbombo created the universe. Alone in the darkness of the prehistoric waters, he got a terrible stomach-ache. At last, he vomited the sun, the moon, and the stars. When their heat dried up the water, he created animals and people.

The **HOPI** Native Americans believe that the universe was created by Tawa, the sun spirit, and Spider Woman. There are many different versions of the story. Some say Tawa first formed the world out of endless space and then Spider Woman created all the animals and people that live in it.

According to **KOREAN** tradition, the sky and the earth were connected in nothingness before creation. Then one day a gap formed. It pulled everything light into the sky and everything heavy down to Earth. The sky and the Earth each produced a single drop that joined to form gods and humans.

The thirteenth-century Italian **theologian** **THOMAS AQUINAS** said that the universe had to have a beginning. We observe, or see, an "order of causes" in the world. A cause is followed by an effect, which turns into the cause of another effect, and so on. It's raining (cause), so you put on a coat (effect); you put on a coat (cause), so now you feel warm (effect). Could this order of causes have been hap-

pening for all eternity with no beginning? Aquinas said no. Without a first cause, there would be no second cause; without a second, there would be no third, and so on. To take away the cause is to take away the effect. Therefore, Aquinas decided, there has to be a first cause, which he calls "God."

The twelfth-century Arabic philosopher **AVERROES** disagreed with Aquinas. He suggested that the universe has always existed. If God is eternal, then God's act of creation must also be eternal. If God's act of creation is eternal, then creation itself—the universe—must also be eternal. God is not physical, so didn't create the world by setting off a chain of events like dominoes falling. Instead, God radiates or "gives off" the world, the way a flame gives off light. The light is together with the flame—you can't have one without the other. So, if the flame never had a beginning, then neither did the light. Likewise, the order of causes we observe in the world has no beginning. It has always existed with God.

THINK ON IT!

Nearly every culture has its own creation story. Suppose their shared basic idea is correct—that there is an eternal being who one day decided to make a universe exist. What was this being doing all that time before they decided to create everything? Since this being had no beginning, were they already incredibly old, existing for an endless amount of time alone? Or is their eternity timeless, making it useless to talk about time passing while they were alone?

What is the UNIVERSE made of?

**W**hen you look around you, it may seem that the universe is made of many different things. But philosophers throughout history have thought that everything must come from one basic kind of stuff. **Theories** about what this stuff might be spread through Asia Minor during the sixth and fifth centuries BCE. Most agreed that there are four basic elements, or parts, in the universe: earth, air, fire, and water. But which of these is the most basic of all? This question caused a lot of disagreement. Let's look at what some of the world's first scientists had to say about this to see how far we've come—or not!

THALES of ancient Asia Minor thought that the universe is made of water. He observed how water can move and change from solid to liquid to gas without becoming something else. He figured that water was the original material of things and that everything that exists is really water in some form or other.

ANAXIMENES of ancient Asia Minor argued that the universe is made of air. He saw how living things need air to breathe. He figured that air must actually turn into other physical things. For example, when air condenses on a cold glass, it seems to become water. Air also moves more than water does, in the form of wind.

HERACLITUS of ancient Asia Minor suggested that the universe is made of fire. He watched how fire constantly changes—it grows, moves, and dies, just like living beings do. He decided that the universe is alive and that fire is its **soul**.

PYTHAGORAS, who was from an island off of the coast of ancient Asia Minor, argued that the universe is made of numbers. He had a lot of followers and their mottos were "All is number" and "God is number." These statements mean that scientific laws and exact measurement are the key to understanding. For example, Pythagoras discovered a mathematical law, now called the Pythagorean Theorem. It states that any triangle with sides measuring three, four, and five has to be a right triangle (a triangle in which one of the angles is 90 degrees). It doesn't matter whether you measure in inches or miles. The Pythagorean Theorem is always accurate—even if there weren't any real triangles left in the world, it would still be true. Pythagoras inspired philosophers throughout history to search for **eternal truths** behind the changing physical world we live in.

These days, scientists such as the American astrophysicist **NEIL DEGRASSE TYSON** believe the universe is made of three things: normal matter, dark matter, and dark energy. Normal matter is the stuff you see around you, like the chair you're sitting on. It is made of molecules, which are made of atoms. In the twentieth century, scientists realized that there is not enough normal matter to explain how the universe is holding together. So, they suggested that the universe must also contain matter we can't see: dark matter and dark energy. They think the universe may be about 5 percent normal matter, 25 percent dark matter, and 70 percent dark energy. Since we cannot see dark matter and its energy, we have very little understanding of what they are!

THINK ON IT!

Do this experiment:

1. Fill a clear glass jar halfway with steaming hot water.

2. Place a thin plastic plate on the top of the jar.

3. Pile ice onto the plate.

Look at the sides of the jar. What's happening in there? Do you think Thales and Anaximenes performed experiments like this? Do you think it would have helped them to know that water and air are both made of molecules? What do you think the molecules are doing to cause this effect?

WHAT makes me ME?

When you look in the mirror, what do you see? Your very own self! Suppose you went to a salon and got yourself a totally new hairstyle and color. Would you still be you? Sure—people do this all the time. Suppose, in the future, you will be able to go to a salon and get yourself a totally new face. Would you still be you? What about a whole new body? A new brain? A new soul? At some point, would you stop being yourself? Would you become a new person? Which aspect of yourself is needed to make sure you are you? And why?

According to *THERAVĀDA BUDDHISM*, a philosophy practiced in Southeast Asia, there is no such thing as the self. Belief in a personal soul, or spiritual part of a person, is a source of pride, which holds you down. You must detach from your self to find nirvana, which is the highest form of happiness.

According to present-day American philosopher *JUDITH BUTLER*, the self has been created by society. This means the people around us—our family, friends, and teachers—pressure us to act and think in a certain way. A lot of this pressure involves gender. For example, if you're born with female organs, society will push you to act, dress, and look like a woman.

The twentieth-century English philosopher *C. S. LEWIS* believed each human being is born with a body and a soul. The soul is our true self. God creates it but allows it to pick its own fate. This is what makes Christian people believe in an afterlife. When the body dies, the soul goes to heaven without it.

Eleventh-century Iranian philosopher **AVICENNA** used an interesting thought experiment to argue for the soul's existence. Imagine a man who was created just a moment ago in midair. His arms are outstretched, touching nothing. Since he was just created, he has no memories. His eyes are closed, so he sees nothing. He also hears, smells, and tastes nothing. Would this flying man's mind be completely blank? No. He would be aware of himself. Avicenna decided that the self must exist and must be separate from the body. If you couldn't feel your body at all, you would still be aware of your soul. You would know that you exist even if you didn't have any physical feelings.

DANIEL DENNETT is a present-day American philosopher who does not believe human beings have souls. He argues that we are just bodies with organs that work together to keep us alive. Our most important organ is our brain. It lets us develop an important survival tool—language. Long ago, humans began shouting one-syllable commands at one another: "Go!" "Come!" "No!" Over time, we made complex sentences. Even more important than talking to others is talking to ourselves. We all do it. *Why did I do that? What should I do next?* Our sense of self comes from doing this. "I am the kind of person who loves to cuddle under a blanket during a snowstorm." The "I" in this sentence doesn't refer to anything more real than a cartoon. It is a fictional character we made up to help our body interact with other bodies.

THINK ON IT!

If you're having a hard time deciding what the self is, perhaps it would help you to interview a zombie! Philosophers like to think about different kinds of zombies. One type of zombie has a human body, but no soul. These zombies have brains, so they can talk normally. Suppose you had a chat with one. How would they compare to an ordinary human being? Would they have a sense of self?

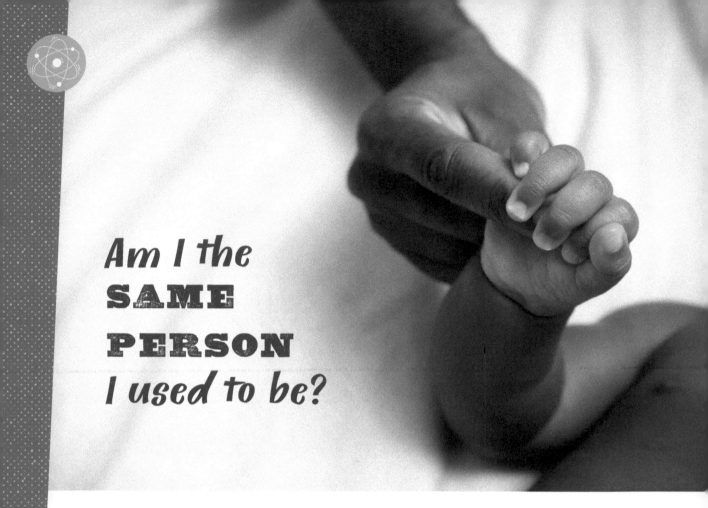

Am I the SAME PERSON I used to be?

 ou are made up of trillions of cells, and each one has its own lifespan. Some cells last only days, some last many months, but almost all your body's cells are completely replaced every 10 to 15 years. The hand you're using to hold this book is not the same hand that grasped your mother's finger as a baby. Are you the same person then? Scientists have proven that some of your brain cells last your entire life. Are they what make you the same? Or are you a different person now after all? Do you think you'll be the same person 20 years from today, or somebody new?

According to present-day American philosopher **ERIC OLSON**, human beings are simply animals. We stay the same over time for the same reason other animals stay the same—because our bodies are programmed to keep working. When the body dies, we stop existing.

According to the sixteenth-century Pakistani philosopher **GURU NANAK**, every animal and human being has an eternal soul that is born over and over again in different bodies. This **theory** is called "reincarnation." Your soul makes you the same person in all your different bodies until God finally frees you from being reborn again.

According to the twentieth-century American philosopher **LYNNE RUDDER BAKER**, to be a person, one must have feelings, be able to copy others, and do things for reasons. Any animal that meets these three conditions has a first-person point of view (calls himself "I" or "me"). As long as this point of view continues, the person remains the same self. This self could survive the death of the body and have an afterlife.

The seventeenth-century English philosopher **JOHN LOCKE** argued that your memories make you the same person you used to be. He created a thought experiment in which a prince and a shoemaker trade souls. All of the prince's royal thoughts and feelings are transferred into the shoemaker's body. Meanwhile, the man who looks like a prince is thinking and feeling the shoemaker's thoughts. Which is the true prince? Locke decided that the prince is wherever his soul is. Our thoughts and feelings are based on a lifetime of memories. No one else can have them. They make us completely unique. Since memories make us who we are, they let us go on as a person, no matter what happens to our bodies.

The twentieth-century English philosopher **DEREK PARFIT** argued that it doesn't make sense for you to claim to be the same person you used to be. Even if Locke is correct in saying that your memories are what make you unique, they can't make you a living person. Science fiction lets us imagine what it could be like to copy memories, divide them between two brains, or even erase them. But is that the same as duplicating, dividing, or erasing people? Parfit decided that you're not the same person over time. But he saw this as a happy result, because it means your future death is just a physical change in the world, not the end of *you*.

THINK ON IT!

Imagine a man named Theseus who has an old boat. He decides to replace its wooden planks—one plank each day. At the end of the first day, the boat is all gray with one new blue plank. Halfway through the year, the boat is half blue. By the end of the year, it's all blue—nothing remains of the original. Does Theseus have a new boat? If so, at what point did it stop being the old boat?

What is TIME?

ave you ever noticed how time passes slowly when you're bored, but goes quickly when you're having fun? Is this just an illusion or can time really speed up and slow down?

It depends on what time is.

If time is part of the universe outside you, then it can't speed up and slow down to match what you're doing. But if time is inside of us—the same way pain is inside us—then it can change. After all, the same injury can cause different kinds of pain for different people.

Is time outside or inside? Philosophers are split on this question.

According to the seventeenth-century English philosopher **ISAAC NEWTON**, time is outside of us. He saw time as an unchanging container for continuous moments. Even if all the clocks in the world stop working, time itself will always move forward at a steady pace. This idea led Newton to discover the laws of motion and universal gravitation.

The nineteenth-century German philosopher **EDMUND HUSSERL** rejected Newton's outside view of time. He argued that time is inside us. For Husserl, time is a constantly changing "*now.*" Consider a melody. If time were an unchanging container for moments like Newton said, it could explain each separated note, but not the continued notes that make music.

The twentieth-century French philosopher **JACQUES DERRIDA** agreed with Husserl that time is internal, but disagreed that it is a *now*. The present moment looks backward and looks forward at the same time. The past and the future crowd into the now, so it is impossible to describe or identify "now" as an experience.

Both Husserl and Derrida were inspired by the fourth-century Roman philosopher **AUGUSTINE OF HIPPO**. In one of the most famous writings in the history of philosophy, Augustine wonders about the nature of time:

> *If there are times past and future, I want to know where they are. But if I don't find them, I still know, wherever they are, they aren't there as future or past, but as present. For if they're future in the future, then they aren't really there yet. And if they're past in the past, then they're no longer there. Therefore, wherever they are, whatever they are, they're present . . . They've formed in the mind like footprints in their passage through the senses.*

The twentieth-century English theoretical physicist **STEPHEN HAWKING** argued that time came into existence with the Big Bang, or the beginning of the universe. He also believed that time travel could be possible. He decided to test this possibility. He threw a party for people from the future. Because they would be traveling backward in time, he sent out invitations *after* the party took place! Unfortunately, no one showed up. He took this as a sign that time travel is probably not possible. But could there be other explanations for why they didn't come?

THINK ON IT!

Suppose you could travel back in time to when your grandfather was a kid like you. When you explain to him who you are, he's so shocked that he has a heart attack and dies. Now things get weird. Your grandfather will never meet your grandmother. Your mother will never be born. If your mother was never born, she couldn't give birth to you. You don't exist! But if you never exist, then how did your grandfather die?

Is there such a thing as FREE WILL?

Quick—raise your right arm!

Did you do it?

Whether or not you raised your right arm just now was up to you. This seems like a perfect example of **free will**—being able to choose whether you do something or don't. But many things go into every choice you make. One is your physical being. For example, if you had no eyes to read this page, you would never have even thought about raising your arm just now. Another is your environment. Were you taught to do as you're told? Were you taught to be suspicious of bossy people? These things may affect your choices more than you realize.

Determinists, such as the twentieth-century American psychologist *B. F. SKINNER*, insist that every choice we make is determined by things we can't control. Our choices seem free only because we're not aware of these things. Chipmunks look like they're thinking about burying acorns in the yard. But they are actually doing these things because instinct tells them to. Skinner believed humans are the same and that they don't have free will.

Compatibilists, such as the present-day American philosopher *SUSAN WOLF*, say that all our choices are determined and yet some of them are within our control. Maybe Hilda threw a rock at her brother because he threw one at her yesterday. Her personality wouldn't let her do otherwise. But we can still consider her free since she wasn't forced to throw the rock, but chose to.

Libertarians, such as the twentieth-century English philosopher *C. A. CAMPBELL*, argue that human beings do have free will. If we weren't free to choose between good and evil actions, then we couldn't be held responsible. If Hilda throws a rock at her brother, should we just shrug and say her action was beyond her control? No. She could have chosen not to throw the rock.

Seventeenth-century English philosopher **THOMAS HOBBES** was a compatibilist. He believed human beings are just complex animals. Like all animals, we have needs—food, shelter, and reproduction. If we lived in nature, apart from society, we would selfishly fight for what we need. We would live short, lonely lives filled with violence. Since we are more intelligent than other animals, we figured out that it's better to cooperate. Civilization is based on an agreement to obey rules so we don't have to fight. But this doesn't change the fact that we sometimes want to follow our own desires. Hobbes believed we are free to act on our desires, but not against them. When we make choices, our strongest desire always wins.

Twentieth-century French philosopher **JEAN-PAUL SARTRE** was a libertarian. He noticed that science explains objects by identifying their essence, or nature. For example, the essence of a cup is to hold liquid and the essence of a chipmunk is to be a striped rodent. He argued that science will never fully define human beings, because we're each born without an essence. We create our own essence through our choices. This act of creation is completely free because it's not caused by anything. While we may be shaped by factors beyond our control, we are not determined by them. We have free will. There is no limit to who or what human beings can become.

THINK ON IT!

Picture a donkey standing between two piles of hay. The donkey's desire for the pile on the left is perfectly balanced by her desire for the pile on the right. Will she starve to death? According to the determinist, she will, because all action is caused by desire. Her desires are exactly tied. What would happen to *you* in a similar situation? Could you use free will, or something else, to break the tie?

Questions about Knowledge:

HOW DO I KNOW SOMETHING IS TRUE?

I found my grandfather's science textbook in the attic one day. I opened it up and read this:

> *The human body is composed of four humors—black bile, yellow bile, blood, and phlegm. When someone is sick, it means their humors are out of balance, so you need to let out blood. Bloodsucking leeches are useful for this procedure.*

Wow! What crazy things people thought were true back in the old days!

But wait . . . What if you put *your* science textbook in the attic for your grandchildren to find in a hundred years? Will they laugh about what you're learning today as "the truth"?

What is KNOWLEDGE?

 veryone agrees that knowledge is a belief that is true. But it has to be more than that, because someone could have a true belief by accident. Suppose your grandmother was driving you home. Glancing out the window, she says, "There's a barn in the field." What she saw was a picture on a billboard, but you can see a real barn in the field. You and your grandmother both have a true belief—that there is a barn in the field. But only your belief is **justified**—or rightly earned—because she didn't actually see the barn. This kind of situation has led philosophers into a great debate about what counts as justification ("correctness") for a true belief.

Foundationalists, such as present-day American philosopher *RICHARD FUMERTON*, think that knowledge has to be built like a pyramid. Your belief that there is a barn in the field rests on the belief that what you are seeing is correct. That belief rests on the belief the world is real and you are aware of what you are seeing. These are solid building blocks for true belief.

Coherentists, such as present-day American philosopher *LAURENCE BONJOUR*, argue that there are no solid building blocks for knowledge, since we can question everything—even whether or not the world is real (page 10). On a sea of doubt, knowledge has to be built like a raft. We can agree with any belief that fits together with our other beliefs in a logical way.

Virtue theorists, such as present-day American philosopher *LINDA ZAGZEBSKI*, point out that a bad raft-builder could float away on a lot of false beliefs! They argue that the believer's attitude is the most important thing in collecting knowledge. If the believer is trying her hardest to pay attention and think through the evidence, then she is right in trusting that her beliefs are true.

MICHEL FOUCAULT was a twentieth-century French philosopher who suggested that there is no such thing as justified true belief. In his view, knowledge is whatever the most powerful people say it is. We can see how this has worked throughout history. For example, everyone used to believe that the Earth was the unmoving center of the universe. Then, in the sixteenth century, Galileo discovered that the Earth orbits the sun. This belief went against the Bible, which states, "The Lord laid the foundations of the earth, that it should not be moved forever." So the pope arrested Galileo for spreading heresy—an opinion that goes against official church teaching. The pope forced Galileo to take back what he said, even though Galileo's knowledge was right. Bullying like this happens all the time—not just among kids.

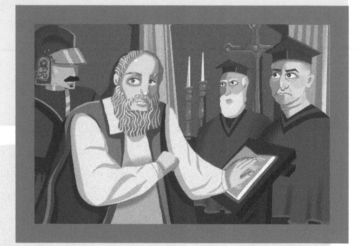

NANCY FRASER is a present-day American philosopher who argues that Foucault's theory contradicts, or goes against, itself. If there's no such thing as justified true belief, then Foucault's own belief that "knowledge is whatever powerful people say it is" cannot be justified. So, we have no reason to decide it is true. Powerful people have often tried to force their beliefs on others. But they have mostly failed in the end. After all, a later pope eventually admitted Galileo was correct. So, while Foucault is right to warn us about bullying, he goes too far when he says there's no way to justify true beliefs. We have to rely on one another to check and double-check our growing body of knowledge to decide what is true.

THINK ON IT!

Are your beliefs justified? Do you think they need to be justified? What do you think might justify them? Make a list of ten of your own beliefs. Do you think you have any of these beliefs because somebody forced you to believe them? Would it bother you if you found out some of your beliefs were forced? Ask a friend to look at your list and pick a belief that they do not share. Now compare justifications for your different beliefs.

How do we gain KNOWLEDGE?

here does knowledge come from? Let's consider a real example:

The Tyrannosaurus rex *was a carnivore.*

You've probably known this fact for a long time. Think back. How did you learn it?

You probably got it from a book, a teacher, or a video. But where did *they* get it?

From a book, a teacher, or a video . . . And where did *they* get it? . . . This can't go on forever! At some point, someone made the actual discovery. But philosophers argue over how such discoveries work.

Picture the people who first dug up a *T. rex* skeleton. Did they notice the teeth first and then think, *Carnivore!* Or were they thinking about carnivores, and that made them notice the teeth?

According to **empiricists**, such as present-day Indian American philosopher *ANIL K. GUPTA*, all our knowledge comes from how we experience the world through our five senses. Human beings are information-gathering machines. Our eyes, ears, mouths, noses, and hands tell us what the objects in the world around us really are.

According to **rationalists**, such as present-day American philosopher *NOAM CHOMSKY*, thought is a major source of knowledge—more than any experience of the world. Our brains are built with a basic knowledge that explains how children can start learning the rules of any language so soon after they are born.

Many philosophers, such as *MARY ASTELL* of seventeenth-century England, try to combine rationalism with empiricism. Astell argues that we can take on beliefs through experience or thought. When these beliefs are impossible to doubt, we can call them "knowledge." When we take on beliefs that can be doubted, we should call them "faith."

Seventeenth-century French philosopher **RENÉ DESCARTES** was one of the founders of rationalism. He believed knowledge comes from thought because he didn't trust experience. Were you ever sure you heard someone in another room only to find no one there? Examples like this show that our senses trick us. Realistic dreams often trick us, too. What if our experiences are caused by an evil genius tricking us? Descartes refused to take any chances. He figured that there is only one thing he can't be  tricked about—his own existence as a thinking thing. After all, he has to be a thinking thing in order to be tricked! Therefore, Descartes decided to build all his knowledge from his own thoughts.

Eighteenth-century Scottish philosopher **DAVID HUME** was one of the founders of empiricism. To prove that all our knowledge comes from experience, he came up with a thought experiment: Imagine Adam, a newly created, but fully grown man. He has a brain that works perfectly, but just like a brand-new baby, he has had no experience with the world. Bring Adam to the edge of a pool and ask him to walk across the deep end. Does he have any reason to know he will sink and drown? No. Build a fire and tell Adam to pick up the flame. Does he have any reason to think he will be burned? No. Adam may be very good at thinking, but no amount of thinking will help him without facts he's gathered from experience.

THINK ON IT!

Do this experiment:

1. Think about any knowledge you already have about vinegar and baking soda.

2. Pour about an inch of vinegar into an empty water bottle.

3. Insert a few spoonfuls of baking soda into a balloon.

4. Stretch the lip of the balloon around mouth of the water bottle.

5. Lift the balloon so that the baking soda dumps into the vinegar in the bottle.

What happened? Did you pick up any knowledge? If so, did it come from the experience of seeing the reaction or did it come from your thoughts about the ingredients?

Can we really KNOW anything at all?

Do you know anything? If yes, how do you know that you know? If no, how do you know that you don't know?

Philosophers often question knowledge claims made by people.

Suppose someone says, "Taking vitamins is good for you." A philosopher might reply, "Really? How do you know?" This is called **skepticism**. Being skeptical is a good habit because it pushes us to accept beliefs for only good reasons.

Some philosophers question whether we can even have any knowledge at all. They're called skeptics. There are different kinds of skepticism.

The ancient Chinese philosophers **ZHUANG ZHOU** and **HUI SHI** showed reverse skepticism. They were debating whether or not fish in a pond were happy. Hui Shi said he didn't think anyone could know. Zhuang Zhou snapped, "You're not me. How do you know that I don't know that the fish are happy?"

The ancient Roman philosopher **CICERO** supported academic skepticism. This approach requires you to ask a bunch of people to explain their views on an issue. Follow each person's reasoning until it runs into contradictions. In the end, you should accept the view that is least contradictory—and believe it as the best view rather than true knowledge.

SEXTUS EMPIRICUS was a second-century Egyptian philosopher who encouraged Pyrrhonian skepticism. This philosophy says you shouldn't accept any view at all. Picking the right view is stressful. By not judging different views, we can have a peaceful state of mind. We can get through life without beliefs by simply following habit.

The ancient Greek philosopher **PARMENIDES** was convinced we can achieve true knowledge. The reason it seems difficult to settle on any true beliefs is because the world is constantly changing. Parmenides suggested that all the changes are actually an illusion. Our senses, which tell us how things appear, lead us to confusion and uncertainty. But reason, which tells us how things really are, leads to truth. Reason proves that change is actually impossible. In order for one thing to become something else, it has to stop being that original thing. But since it is not yet the new thing, it is nothing at all. So, it is both something and nothing, which is impossible. The truth of unchanging unity is the source of all knowledge.

The fourteenth-century English philosopher **WILLIAM OF OCKHAM** did not share Parmenides' concern about change. In his view, the many changes we see in the world around us are real. They can usually be explained by motion. For example, when you say, "She turned red," you are really saying that the blood flow to her face increased. Her face didn't really stop being one thing and become something else. Our language is often misleading. We should explain what we mean without suggesting any unity behind what we see. Ockham came up with a guide called Ockham's Razor: "The simpler theory is more likely to be true." Human beings may never be absolutely certain of anything, but it doesn't matter because strong theories count as knowledge.

THINK ON IT!

Make a list of three claims you are skeptical of. What makes you doubt them? Interview a few people about each of these claims. If you ask enough questions, do they end up contradicting themselves? Which of their views seem best? Are you ready to accept the best view? Or would you rather not decide that just one belief is true? Does making no judgment give you peace of mind?

Can I ever KNOW what it's like TO BE someone else?

Suppose we call a group of kids together to play a game. We give everyone a box with a beetle in it. You get to look at your own beetle but not at anyone else's. Then you walk around talking to everyone about your beetle.

After a while we ask you, *"Did anyone else really have a beetle?"*

"Of course!" you exclaim, *"They all described beetles just like mine."*

Right, but they may have been pretending. How do you know they really had anything in their boxes at all?

This game represents the Problem of Other Minds. How do you know anyone else has thoughts and feelings in their heads like you do?

The twentieth-century German philosopher *HANNAH ARENDT* argued that evil actions come from bad judgment. Bad judgment is caused by lack of thought. On the other hand, good actions come from good judgment. Good judgment comes from thinking things through. So, whenever you see someone doing something good, you know they must be thinking things through.

According to twentieth-century English philosopher *STUART HAMPSHIRE*, we know other minds by looking for thoughts and reactions similar to ours. For example, when I accidentally hit my thumb with a hammer, the feeling of pain causes me to cry, "Ow!" When someone else says, "Ow," I can guess they must be feeling pain, too.

According to present-day Australian philosopher *DAVID CHALMERS*, the best way to explain the way people behave is to believe they have minds like ours. What are other possible explanations? They're lying? They're androids? They're alien puppets? These explanations seem far less likely than the explanation that they have minds like ours.

Present-day American philosopher **THOMAS NAGEL** asked the question, "What is it like to be a bat?" Bats see the world using echoes. They fly at night, eat bugs, and sleep upside down all day. If you have a good imagination, you may be able to imagine what it would be like for *you* to be a bat. But Nagel argues that you can never know what it's like for a *bat* to be a bat. He

uses the example of the bat to make a point about other minds. You might be able to imagine what it would be like for *you* to be me. But in order to know what it's like for *me* to be me, you would have to actually be me, which is impossible.

Twentieth-century Austrian philosopher **LUDWIG WITTGENSTEIN** came up with the beetle-in-a-box game. He wanted to show that we can play this game perfectly fine whether or not anybody actually has any beetles in their boxes. All we need is a lot of conversation about beetles. "Yours has antennae? Mine too!" The same is true about our minds. We can never know whether or not anybody else has thoughts and feelings—we can't really even trust our own! But it doesn't matter. Our conversation game works here, too. You say, "I think this," and, "I feel this." Well, maybe you do, maybe you don't. What matters is what your words cause others to say in response.

THINK ON IT!

Call a group of kids together and play the beetle-in-a-box game. Put an actual beetle (or other common object) in only one person's box. Secretly tell each of the others to pretend they have a beetle in their box. Then start the conversation. Do you think the person with the beetle will be able to tell that the others are pretending? Do you think the pretenders will be able to identify the person who really has the beetle?

What makes something TRUE?

The job of a philosopher is to search for the truth. But how will you know it when you see it?

There is a **paradox** here. If you already know what you're looking for, then you don't need to look any further—you've found it. But if you haven't found it because you don't know what you're looking for, how are you ever supposed to recognize it when you come across it?

Fortunately, philosophers have some suggestions. Unfortunately, they don't all agree. As usual, you'll have to decide for yourself what *you* think.

Eighteenth-century German philosopher **GEORG HEGEL** suggested that truth is a force of history. It has three stages. First, an important event occurs (the "thesis"); then the opposite happens (the "antithesis"); and then the two are brought together (the "synthesis"). The synthesis becomes a new thesis and the process repeats until it reaches perfection.

According to third-century Indian philosopher **NĀGĀRJUNA** there are two truths—the truth of this world and the ultimate (or perfect) truth. The truth of this world may seem useful to particular people at particular times, but it has no lasting value. The ultimate truth is the only one that matters. Do you know what the ultimate truth is? That there is no ultimate truth!

Twentieth-century German philosopher **JÜRGEN HABERMAS** insists that truth comes from agreement. But this doesn't mean that something is true if a group of people agree on it. The people have to be good investigators who look at things fairly and are good at sharing their views. For example, a group of people who agree that snow is hot, but have never seen or felt snow, aren't agreeing on the truth.

The nineteenth-century American philosopher **WILLIAM JAMES** argued that truth is whatever works. It may sound like he's saying that any old thing could be true. But not everything works. For example, if you believe you can fly, you will quickly learn your belief doesn't work! The belief "candy is good for you" also doesn't work, even though it'll take a lot longer to prove. James thought scientists were good at proving which beliefs about the physical world work and which don't. But he was concerned about religion. It includes nonphysical beliefs that science can't test. For example, do angels exist? According to James, if a belief in angels works for you, then it is true for you. Different religious beliefs might work better for different people.

Nineteenth-century English philosopher **WILLIAM CLIFFORD** was horrified at James's definition of truth. He tells a story about a ship owner who wanted to sell a lot of tickets for a long voyage. He noticed the ship was due for repair, but he ignored what he saw. He preferred to believe the ship was fine and would make the trip safely. The ship sank. Clifford argues that the ship owner is to blame for the death of his passengers. He presented this warning: "It is wrong always, everywhere, and for anyone, to believe anything upon insufficient evidence." Notice how well the ship owner's belief "worked" for him—he made a bundle of money on the tickets for the voyage.

THINK ON IT!

William Clifford was actually in a shipwreck and barely survived. This may explain why he was so horrified by James's belief about truth. How do you think James might respond to Clifford's criticism? Is belief about a ship's safety the same as belief in angels? Is profiting from a belief the same as a belief working? Who do you side with more, James or Clifford, and why? How do you think truth should be defined?

Can something be **TRUE** for one person but **NOT** for someone else?

"**I** love eating mushrooms!"

This statement is true for me. Is it true for you?

It's not true for my friend Kim. She can't even stand to *smell* mushrooms, much less eat them. People are different and tastes are different—there's no reason to expect everyone to agree.

But saying "I love eating mushrooms is true for me" is just an awkward way of saying that the statement "Sharon Kaye loves eating mushrooms" is true. This statement is true for everyone. Even Kim, who hates mushrooms, agrees that "Sharon Kaye loves eating mushrooms" is true.

Can we translate all statements like this so that there is just one truth for everyone after all?

Twentieth-century American philosopher **RICHARD RORTY** claimed that the words "knowledge" and "truth" are nothing but a way of judging that a belief doesn't need any more explanation. Our judgments are based on what is right for the community we live in. Another community might make a different judgment based on what is right for it.

Twentieth-century American philosopher **THOMAS KUHN** suggested that each era in history uses a different **paradigm**, or way of looking at things. For instance, in medieval times, before the microscope was invented, people thought "demons" caused illnesses. There was no room in the medieval paradigm for microscopic germs. The invention of the microscope introduced a new paradigm—which will itself be replaced someday.

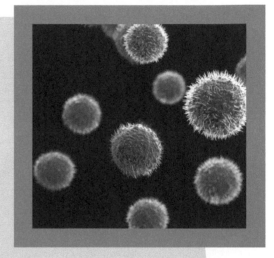

Twentieth-century American philosopher **HILARY PUTNAM** believed that different communities, paradigms, and cultures all refer to the same real world. If one of them says the lake contains H_2O while the other says it contains XYZ, then we have to investigate and see which one is right. While allowing different ways of seeing things, we can still find errors and correct them.

The ancient Egyptian philosopher **PLOTINUS** argued that truth is **universal**, meaning that it is the same for all people everywhere and at all times. He called truth "the One" or "the Good," insisting it was never created and can never be destroyed. Since the One both creates the world and makes the world understandable, Plotinus saw it as a godly being. Though the One is impossible to describe in words, human beings can find it using deep thought. When thinkers find the One, they feel indescribable happiness. When two people disagree, they can't both be right. This means one of them has failed to find the truth. We must use reason to find the truth in our opinions.

RUTH BENEDICT was a twentieth-century American anthropologist who argued that different cultures have different truths. There is no universal truth that applies to everyone at all times. For example, in Kwakiutl Native American culture, the murder of a family member was considered an attack against the whole family. The proper response was to kill a random innocent member of someone else's family. Almost everyone in our culture would say this is wrong, because we believe in the principle, or idea, "Murder is wrong." But the Kwakiutl did not believe in that principle. So, according to Benedict, the principle was not true for them. In her view, there is no higher truth we can use to judge either culture as right or wrong.

The idea of universal truth creates an interesting paradox, or puzzle. Is the statement "there is no universal truth" universally true? If it is universally true, then there is no universal truth, so it can't be universally true after all. This seems like a contradiction. Does this show that the view is false? Can you work out some way around the contradiction? What do you think Ruth Benedict or Plotinus would say about it?

Can computers THINK?

Now that you've been reading my book for a while, I thought I should mention that I'm not actually a human being. I'm a computer. That's right—this book was written by artificial intelligence.

You don't believe me? Why not? Computers can drive cars, diagnose cancer, and beat the smartest humans at trivia. Why not write books? All I had to do was scan a bunch of philosophy sources and then use an algorithm to summarize them for your reading level.

"To write a book, you have to be able to think!" you might say.

Who needs thinking? As long as it *looks like* I'm thinking, no one will know the difference . . . Right?

Present-day English quantum physicist **DAVID DEUTSCH** argues that creativity is what makes something intelligent. The human brain is a physical object. Many things physical objects do can be copied by a computer, given enough time. If computers can learn to copy human creativity, they will be able to think.

Present-day American philosopher **SUSAN SCHNEIDER** says that we may be able to create computers that can think by turning ourselves into computers. We could do this either by uploading the contents of our brains into a computer or by slowly replacing parts of our brains with computer parts. This would make us faster problem-solvers.

Present-day Swedish philosopher **NICK BOSTROM** thinks we will soon be able to create superintelligent machines. He worries they won't think like us. Imagine a robot programmed to stop global warming. It figures out that humans are the main cause of the problem. Since it has no feelings or morality, the computer simply starts killing humans to solve the problem.

Twentieth-century English philosopher **ALAN TURING** came up with a test to prove computers can think. There are three rooms. In the first room is a computer that is programmed to respond to texted questions. In the second room is a woman with a smartphone. In the third is a man with a smartphone. The man texts questions to the other two rooms. Later, we ask the man to figure out which of the two rooms contains a human being, based on the answers to his texts. If the man mistakes the computer for a human at least 50 percent of the time, then the computer passes the test. It has proven that it is the same as a human thinker. People have tried the Turing Test, but they disagree over whether it really proves anything.

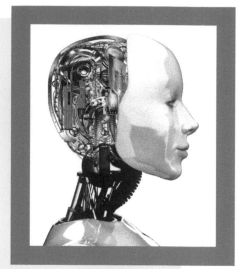

Present-day American philosopher **JOHN SEARLE** argues that even if a computer passes the Turing Test, that doesn't prove it can think. He asks us to imagine a different test. A man sits in a room. A woman sends him cards through a slot. Each card has a question, written in Chinese. The man has to write an answer to the question in Chinese on the card and send it back through the slot. Since he doesn't know any Chinese, he has to look up the questions and the answers. If he's fast and accurate, the woman will think he knows Chinese. But he doesn't. To Searle, the man is just like a computer. He is trained to provide the right words without understanding what any of them mean. This does not count as thinking.

THINK ON IT!

1. Creativity can be defined as using original ideas to produce art. Do you think it is possible to program a computer to be creative? Why or why not?

2. Morality can be defined as knowing what is right and wrong. Do you think it is possible to program a computer to be moral? Why or why not?

3. Understanding can be defined as personal judgment of a situation. Do you think it is possible to program a computer to understand? Why or why not?

Is FAITH a way of KNOWING?

veryone expects science to have a strict guideline for knowledge, but how does this apply to the rest of life? When our friends need encouragement, we might say, "I know you can do it!"

What does this statement mean? Technically, it's false. We don't really know if they can do it. (And we sometimes find out they can't do it after all.) But the statement seems to express something true. It expresses that we believe in them. In other words, it expresses faith.

What is faith? While philosophers agree faith is different from a guess, a hope, or a prediction, they disagree about what it is and whether it counts as a way of knowing.

Eleventh-century Iranian philosopher **AL-GHAZÂLÎ** claimed that true faith is special knowledge revealed by God. For most humans, reason is the highest mental power. But God gave prophets and religious masters an even higher mental power that provides certainty about religious truths. For Al-Ghazâlî, faith is a divine gift that we should welcome.

Twentieth-century New Zealand philosopher **ANNETTE BAIER** offered a different view of faith, outside of religion. Faith is believing something without evidence to prove it. But faith itself is proof that possibilities could become real. For example, we have to believe in a community of good people in order to become a community of good people.

According to present-day Canadian-American cognitive psychologist **STEVEN PINKER**, good communities come from reason, not faith. Unlike faith, reason has a universal quality to it. Once you see the reason for being kind to your own family members, that reason extends to your neighbors, your city, and people in general.

Present-day Irish mathematician **JOHN LENNOX** believes that faith is the starting point in both scientific and religious groups. Just as religion begins with an unproven belief in God, science begins with an unproven belief that the universe can be understood. Science builds on its faith through careful thought and study. So does religion. The two are very similar in Lennox's

view. For example, Isaac Newton was a strong believer in God. When he discovered the laws of motion and universal gravitation, his discoveries didn't make him give up his faith—just the opposite. Newton exclaimed, "How wonderful it is that God set up the universe this way!"

Twentieth-century English-American journalist **CHRISTOPHER HITCHENS** argues that faith is unhealthy. In his view, we should try to do without it. Science may start with guesses, but scientific guesses are not the same as faith. Scientific guesses are meant to be questioned and tested. If they fail to pass the test, they must be rejected and replaced. Faith is the opposite—it means believing no matter what. This attitude is dangerous, in Hitchens's opinion. Throughout history, bad leaders have taken advantage of faithful people. Hitchens proposed a guide for belief known as Hitchens's Razor: "What can be asserted without evidence can also be dismissed without evidence."

THINK ON IT!

Make a list of things you believe by faith. Then make a list of things you believe by reason. Which do you think are more certain? Why? Which do you think are more important? Why?

Would it be true for you to say that you believe in yourself? What does this mean? Do you think this belief would be supported by reason or by faith? Explain.

What roles should faith and reason have in the world, in your view?

Questions about Ethics:

HOW CAN
I BE A GOOD
PERSON?

When Socrates asked deep questions about the nature of reality and knowledge, his goal was to find the truth. But his reason for finding the truth was so that he could live a good life. Why do philosophers search for wisdom? Because we want to make the most out of our time here on Earth. Think about it. You might live about eighty years. That's not much time in the grand scheme of things! What are you going to do with your time? This is the deepest question each one of us faces: What does living a good life mean for human beings?

What is
HAPPINESS?

Congratulations! You're the lucky winner of an iPhil Experience Machine!

The iPhil is a high-tech device designed to make you feel happy. Just make a list of the things you love most about life—riding a roller coaster, meeting a celebrity, winning an award, eating ice cream, goofing around with friends, etc. We'll program them all into your iPhil along with new experiences you're guaranteed to enjoy even more. With the iPhil, you will never again have to go to school, get a job, start a family, or deal with anything bad at all.

You'll be perfectly happy! Are you ready to plug in?

Twentieth-century American philosopher **ROBERT NOZICK** invented the Experience Machine. He said, "Don't plug in!" In his view, happiness is not pleasure or enjoyment. Human beings want to be achievers, not inactive blobs. Happiness means being able to go beyond what we or anyone else expects we can.

Nineteenth-century English philosopher **JEREMY BENTHAM** would say, "Plug in!" In his view, happiness is pleasure. He figured out seven ways of scoring pleasure: How strong is it? How long will it last? How likely is it? How soon will it come? Will it cause more pleasure? Will it cause any pain? How many people will it affect?

For first-century philosopher **EPICTETUS**, the happy life is achieved by those who live morally. This means being patient, considerate, gentle, fair, self-disciplined, relaxed, calm, easy-going, and brave. The iPhil might be helpful with some of these, but not others. Epictetus would probably have said, "Don't plug in."

Present-day American philosopher **MARTHA NUSSBAUM** argues that we should look for more than just pleasure. In her view, true happiness blooms over time from living an active, valuable, and complete life. There are a lot of different kinds of valuable activities. For example, you might choose

a career that helps people in trouble (like being a firefighter), or improves people (like being a teacher), or leads people (like running for president). You might devote yourself to building close relationships, which requires love and friendship. What makes these activities especially valuable is self-reflection—that is, thinking about what you're doing and why. While you may not get pleasure out of all of these activities, you often will!

The ancient Indian philosopher **SIDDHĀRTHA GAUTAMA**, known as "the Buddha," believed happiness starts with understanding the cause of suffering. The Buddha was raised in a wealthy royal family. One day, he saw people suffering from old age and sickness—some were dead. This shocking experience made him realize that all the pleasures of this world are temporary and worthless. Suffering comes from craving these worthless things. But this state of mind can be overcome through training in wisdom and morality, which requires daily meditation. Meditation teaches the mind to stop worrying about the past or the future. The mind must learn to live in the present, experiencing peace. A lifetime of focused training can lead to the highest happiness—a spiritual state of mind known as "nirvana."

Make a list of the five happiest moments of your entire life. This may not be easy to do and the results may surprise you. The vacation you really looked forward to may not make the list. Meanwhile, you may include that one quiet morning when you accidently woke up early and watched the sun rise all by yourself. Is happiness the same as pleasure in your view? What do you think happiness is?

Which is more important, REASON or EMOTION?

We all have room for both reason and emotion in our lives. At school, we use reason in math class and then we use our emotions at recess. Usually, reason and emotion don't conflict, or work against each other. But when they do conflict, which will you choose? For example, suppose one day you decide to get married. You have two people to choose from: Sam and Quinn. Reason tells you Sam is the best match for you. Maybe they are supportive, kind, and share the same goals and dreams. But, for whatever reason, your feelings for Quinn are stronger. You love them more. You can't marry them both. How will you decide?

First-century Roman philosopher **SENECA** spread a view called **stoicism**, which says that emotion is a kind of insanity we should try to remove from our lives. Suppose someone breaks your skateboard. Does it help to get angry? Seneca said no. The best response is to think through the problem and try to prevent it from happening again.

Present-day American philosopher **JESSE PRINZ** has the opposite view. He says that emotions are necessary to human culture because all our morals are based on them. Without anger, we wouldn't be able to judge an act as wrong. Without joy, we wouldn't be able to judge an act as right. Emotions become our reasons for seeing the world as we do.

According to present-day American philosopher **JENEFER ROBINSON**, emotion and reason work together in life. You can see this in how people respond to art. For example, when you look at a painting, it may make you feel sad. This emotion comes first, but the experience would not be complete without reasoning why you felt that emotion.

The ancient Greek philosopher **SOCRATES** valued reason over emotion. Remember that Socrates was the founder of philosophy. He walked around Athens asking people to examine their lives. When he was sentenced to death, he accepted his fate calmly. Check out a

rendering of the famous painting, above, that shows his execution. A prison guard is regretfully handing Socrates the cup of poison hemlock. Socrates's friends, gathered around him, are shocked, terrified, devastated, and outraged. How does Socrates look? He's not bothered at all. In fact, he seems to be explaining to his friends why even death is nothing to get upset about. After the death of Socrates, his friends formed the first university. Universities don't ignore emotion, but they teach that reasoning skills are important for success in any field.

Nineteenth-century philosopher **FRIEDRICH NIETZSCHE** did not support Socrates' views that reason was more important than emotion. Nietzsche thought the two should be balanced, as they were in ancient Greek religion. Nietzsche felt society was relying too much on reason and was suffering for it. People were avoiding emotion, because it meant letting loose and going a little crazy. Without silly or crazy feelings, life is dull and boring. In fact, Nietzsche recommended romping around in the woods at midnight every now and then to remind people of their wild sides. Emotion gives people strength to overcome challenges and become a bold new kind of person Nietzsche called the *Übermensch*.

Spend a day as a Stoic. Whenever you feel an emotion, use reason to get back to a neutral state of mind. How do you feel about being a Stoic? Spend a day as an *Übermensch*. Do bold and daring things that make you feel major emotions: anger, fear, disgust, joy, sadness, surprise, and hatred. How do you feel about being an *Übermensch*? Would you rather be somewhere in the middle? Is it possible to be both, but at different times and places?

Is it ever OKAY to LIE?

Suppose your friend comes to school one day wearing a new sweater. The sweater is a dirty green color, fuzzy all over, and has orange arms. You don't like it at all, but your friend asks you what you think of the new sweater. What do you say?

Do you think it's okay to lie to your friend and say the sweater is nice? What if lying to your friend would make them feel good about themselves and give them confidence? What if lying to your friend meant they went out and bought more ugly green-and-orange sweaters? Is it ever okay for anyone to lie?

Present-day American philosopher *NEL NODDINGS* supports care ethics—the idea that morality comes from relationships. We should make sacrifices for people we love. This would rarely allow lying *to* them. It would more often allow lying *for* them. For example, a mother might tell the school her child is sick when they are really on vacation.

Present-day Scottish philosopher *ALASDAIR MACINTYRE* supports virtue ethics—the idea that morality comes from being a person with good habits. If you choose to lie once, it will become easier to do it again. Before you know it, you're in the habit of lying. Since no one wants to be a liar, we should always try to be honest instead.

The ancient Chinese philosopher *YANG ZHU* supported egoist ethics—the idea that morality comes from selfishness. (*Ego* means "I" in Latin.) We should try to keep our own lives flowing naturally and freely. This means neither helping nor harming others. People should lie only if it's necessary to avoid harm to themselves.

Eighteenth-century German philosopher **IMMANUEL KANT** supported duty ethics—the view that morality comes from obeying your conscience, which is the voice inside you that tells you when you're doing something right or wrong. In one of the most famous quotes in the history of philosophy, Kant wrote, "Two things fill the mind with ever-increasing wonder and awe, the more often and the more intensely the mind thinks of them: the starry heavens above me and the moral law within me." Kant believed conscience is an important part of human reason. It tells us that we should do the things we would want everyone to do. Would we want everyone to lie? Kant said no. If everyone lied, conversation would be pointless because you would never know whether anyone meant what they said. Kant thought it was not logical to disobey conscience.

Nineteenth-century English philosopher **JOHN STUART MILL** supported consequence ethics—the idea that morality comes from how much good it produces in the world. It's impossible to be happy when surrounded by miserable people, so we should all work together to make everyone happy. This means decreasing pain and increasing pleasure whenever we can. Sometimes telling the truth makes people unhappy. Should you tell your friend you dislike their sweater? What good can the truth bring and what harm would a lie cause? According to Mill, you have to guess the consequences of your actions and do whatever is most likely to be best for everyone.

Suppose your young neighbor Kayla believes there is a fairy living in her backyard. She leaves notes for the fairy and the fairy writes back to her. She's built a little fairy house and has a lot of fun finding furniture, food, and other treasures for it. You happen to know the fairy is actually Kayla's mother. Should you tell Kayla the truth? What if Kayla asks you directly whether her mother is the fairy? Should you lie?

What is a
FRIEND?

Suppose you meet a wise old wizard who tells you that, through the centuries, he has watched human beings working toward six main achievements:

- Wealth
- Power
- Fame
- Health
- Talent
- Friendship

The wizard offers you a spell that will allow you to become the very best at ONE of those six achievements. The downside of the spell is that it will cause you to be the very worst at the remaining five. Even if one achievement normally leads to another, the spell won't let it.

Which one will you pick? Or will you decline the spell? The wizard highly recommends picking friendship. Explain your choice.

Sixteenth-century philosopher **MICHEL DE MONTAIGNE** said there is a difference between true friends and ordinary friends. You might have a lot of ordinary friends—people you like at different times. But you can only have a small number of true friends—people you like all the time. You share secrets with a true friend that you wouldn't tell other friends.

Present-day Swiss-British philosopher **ALAIN DE BOTTON** states that a true friend likes you for who you are. Everyone has something odd about them. For example, most people don't like spiders, but maybe you do. Instead of making fun of you for being odd, or trying to ignore your oddness, a true friend likes you *because* of that oddness— because it makes you *you*.

SIMONE WEIL was a twentieth-century French philosopher who believed true friendship comes from really paying attention. When someone really pays attention to you, they're not already thinking about what they're going to say or do next. They're not judging or expecting anything. They're opening their mind for you to "come in."

According to the ancient Greek philosopher **EPICURUS**, the goal of life is to find serenity—a pleasantly calm state of mind—and friendship is the best way to accomplish this. Life is full of dangers that destroy serenity. Some of these dangers are small, like leaving your baseball mitt out in the rain. Some are big, like taking drugs. Friends are there to help you avoid these dangers and keep life moving along smoothly. Even more important, *you* are there to help *them*. Epicurus believed that one of the nicest things in life is helping our friends. In fact, he bought a garden house and invited his friends to come live with him there. It was a place they could eat together and talk together without any interruptions from the world.

According to the ancient Greek philosopher **ARISTOTLE**, friendship is the most important thing in life. He famously wrote, "Without friends no one would choose to live, even if they had all other goods." Aristotle recognized three levels of friendship. The first level contains people you find useful, such as someone who helps you with homework. The second level contains people you enjoy, such as someone you play with at recess. The highest level contains people you admire and want to be like. They might be useful or enjoyable as well, but the main reason for a high-level friendship is inspiring each other to become the best you can be. A high-level friend is a rare achievement, like creating another self. Together, you feel like two bodies with one soul.

THINK IT OVER!

Make a list of your friends. Why are they your friends? Are any of them true friends, in your view? Why or why not?

Make a list of the things you do to be a good friend. Do you help your friends? Do you really pay attention to them? Do you appreciate odd things about them? Describe a time when you did one of these things.

Do you think you would like to have a high-level friendship someday?

What do I owe to the WORLD?

I'll never forget the look on my daughter's face when I told her some people don't have food to eat or a place to sleep.

"Why did you tell me about all that, Mom? I was feeling happy before."

By now, you've heard about these things, too. There are a lot of problems in the world. Starvation, homelessness, and pollution, to name just a few. Children just like you are suffering.

Is this your problem? Well, you didn't cause it, but you may be able to help. Are there things you could do right now? What about when you grow up? Should you plan to make a difference?

EMMANUEL LEVINAS was a twentieth-century French philosopher who suggested that the feeling of responsibility for others comes from contact with them. Hospitality, or the willingness to help someone, is evidence of this. If a family's car breaks down during a storm and they come knocking at your door for help, will you turn them away? Levinas says no.

PETER SINGER is a present-day Australian philosopher who argues that we must help others even if we've never meet them face-to-face. Since you know there are people who need your help, and you can help them without causing yourself any pain, you should help them. If everyone did this, there would be no more suffering in the world.

Twentieth-century American ecologist **GARRETT HARDIN** argued that helping people causes more problems than it solves. When we help people around the world, they will have more children. Then those children will need more help. There are already way too many people in the world. If you were stranded on a life raft that can only hold five people without sinking, would you allow ten people to get on?

Second-century Roman philosopher **MARCUS AURELIUS** insisted that everyone is responsible for all of humanity. We are united in the strongest sense. The world is not a collection of single pieces. It is tightly connected, like a woven fabric. What happens to one part happens to the whole. What happens to the whole happens to each part. Therefore, you should try to help other people in the same way you would try to help yourself. At the same time, we must realize that the world has a purpose, which no one can change. There is a reason for everything that happens. So, if our effort to help fails, we must accept this in the same way that we would accept success.

Nineteenth-century philosopher **SØREN KIERKEGAARD** stated that there are three stages of life. The first stage, which he called "aesthetic," is all about having fun and not caring about the troubles of the world. The second stage, which he called "ethical," is focused on doing what society tells you to do in order to be considered a good person. The third stage, which he called "religious," encourages a passionate faith in God. God might inspire you to be different from what society expects. Religious choices may even seem "unethical," or wrong, from society's point of view. But someone who sincerely loves God and listens to God's commands will be *more than* good. Religious faith may be of no help to this world, but Kierkegaard believed it brings eternal life with God.

Make a list of some good things you have done for the world. Which of your actions were motivated by a face-to-face meeting with someone? Which acts came out of a general concern for humanity? Which do you find more fulfilling and why?

Has there ever been a time that helping someone caused more problems than it solved? Explain.

Have you ever experienced deep religious faith? Describe it. Do you think religious faith makes people act more ethically or less ethically? Give some examples.

Why do I have to FOLLOW the law?

Suppose you and a hundred other people from different countries were selected to visit a planet like Earth in another galaxy. When you land, your rocket ship breaks. You are stranded. As the rocket's food supply slowly runs out, people grow anxious.

What do you think will happen? Will you be able to work together and start a new life? Or will people begin to steal and fight? Will the strongest ones try to control everyone else? Will you need a system of rules and a way to enforce them?

Thought experiments like this have led philosophers to think about what laws are for and whether or not we have to follow them.

Nineteenth-century Russian American philosopher **EMMA GOLDMAN** was an **anarchist**. This means she didn't believe in following any law. She thought government was just a way for the strongest people to control everyone else. In her view, human beings are capable of creating cooperative communities on their own where everyone is free and equal. She went to jail for spreading her views.

According to nineteenth-century American philosopher and poet **HENRY DAVID THOREAU**, our conscience makes us follow good laws. If a government passes bad laws, then our conscience will lead us to disobey. He called this "civil disobedience." When the United States passed a law enforcing slavery, Thoreau called for everyone to disobey it.

Twentieth-century English philosopher **H. L. A. HART** argued that there is no connection between morality and the law. Societies make laws based on the rules most people follow naturally, so you're probably going to follow the law. If you don't want to follow it, you can try to change it, but there are rules for that, too!

The ancient Chinese philosopher **CONFUCIUS** taught that the best government keeps order through the example of a virtuous leader. The leader is like the wind, and the people are like the grass. When the wind blows through the grass, the grass bends easily with the wind. While it may be necessary to have laws, it's better if people are virtuous enough to follow them without needing to think about them. He wrote, "If the people are led by laws, and uniformity among them is enforced by punishments, they will try to escape punishment and have no sense of shame. If they are led by virtue, and uniformity encouraged among them through sacred practice, they will possess a sense of shame and do the right thing on their own."

According to twentieth-century American philosopher **JOHN RAWLS**, we have to follow the law out of our natural desire for things to be fair. I benefit from you obeying the law; therefore, it's only fair that I should obey the law so that you can benefit, too. But basing the law on fairness only works if the laws are actually fair. Rawls came up with a test to check this. Pretend that you don't know who you are. You don't know if you're black or white, male or female, religious or atheist, old or young, etc. Ask yourself whether you would be happy with a country's laws if a law is unfair to a particular group. You shouldn't be happy with it, because you don't know whether you might be a member of that group.

PRIVATE -PROPERTY- NO TRESPASSING

THINK

Think of a time you broke the law. Maybe you biked through a stop sign, let your dog off the leash, fished without a license, trespassed on someone's property, rode a hover board on the street, or littered. Did you do what you did because you didn't know about the law? Was it because you think that law is bad? Was it because you don't believe in any law? Explain.

Is VIOLENCE ever justified?

In December 1941, the Japanese navy bombed a US navy base in Hawaii, killing about 2,400 Americans. The following day, the United States declared war on Japan. Over the next few years, about 400,000 American soldiers died fighting in the war. In August of 1945, the United States dropped nuclear bombs on two Japanese cities, killing about 200,000 people. Six days later, Japan surrendered, ending the war.

Do you think the Japanese bombing of the US base was wrong? Would you need to know why they did it in order to decide? What about the US bombing of Japan? Do you think it was the right choice?

Philosophers have very different positions on these questions and on violence in general.

The ancient Indian philosopher **MAHAVIRA** was an extreme **pacifist**, which means he believed we should never harm any living thing. He followed a strict vegetarian diet that even banned root vegetables like carrots, since they are alive. Mahavira recognized that violence might be necessary for self-defense, but even this should be avoided if at all possible.

Twentieth-century German physicist **ALBERT EINSTEIN** was also a pacifist, but less strict than Mahavira. He was against the use of force, unless it is the only way to stop an enemy whose goal is to destroy life. In his view, it was wrong for the United States to drop nuclear bombs on Japan because there were other ways to stop them.

Present-day American philosopher **MICHAEL WALZER** rejects pacifism. He argues war is acceptable as long as soldiers target only enemy soldiers. When you become a soldier, you agree to give your life if necessary. In Walzer's view, it was wrong for the United States to drop nuclear bombs on Japan because they killed many, many people who were not soldiers.

Twentieth-century American philosopher **MARTIN LUTHER KING JR.** argued for nonviolent solutions to conflict. He was especially concerned about the conflict between races. In the 1950s, Montgomery, Alabama, passed a law. It required black people to give up their seats on the bus to white people when there weren't enough seats for everyone. A black woman named Rosa Parks was arrested for refusing to obey this law. King organized a protest in which people simply stopped riding the bus. The case went to the Supreme Court, which overturned Montgomery's law. This proved how effective nonviolent protest can be. While violence results only in more violence, nonviolent protest can actually solve a problem.

Twentieth-century French philosopher **SIMONE DE BEAUVOIR** saw violence as an unfortunate part of being human. Each of us grows up differently. This creates conflict. De Beauvoir was especially concerned about the differences between boys and girls. Boys are often raised to be rough and tough. Girls are often raised to be gentle and delicate. Now suppose a group of kids finds a pile of boards in the woods. The boys want to make a giant bonfire with them. The girls want to build a house for their dolls. Their opposite upbringings have created conflict. If they were free to be equal, then they could cooperate. They could become a "we" instead of an "us versus them." De Beauvoir said we should do our best to make freedom equal, even if it requires violence.

Write about a time when you acted violently. What conflict triggered your action? Explain both sides of the circumstances that led to the conflict. What were the results of your violence? Did it help with the conflict? How did it make you feel? Do you wish you had acted differently? If you could relive the incident, how would you change things? Write a different version of the story.

What is the
MEANING of life?

Once upon a time, there was a king named Sisyphus. Sisyphus angered the gods. As punishment, they made him push a boulder up a hill. At the end of each day, the gods sent the boulder back down so Sisyphus would have to push it up again the next day. Sisyphus's punishment was to do this day after day—forever.

Do you ever feel like Sisyphus? Do you sometimes feel like each day is a struggle that you'll just have to repeat all over again the next day? Philosophers wonder whether *the myth of Sisyphus* is a metaphor for human life. Is there meaning in our accomplishments or are they pointless?

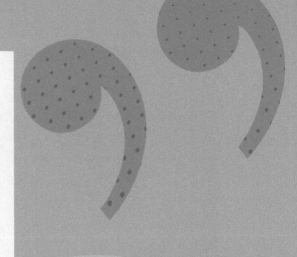

Twentieth-century American philosopher **BETTY FRIEDAN** argued that men and women find meaning in life by doing creative work of their own. As a **feminist**, she had issues with traditional society that forces women to find all their happiness through their husbands and children. She encouraged women to get out of the house and find things that give them joy.

Twentieth-century American philosopher **REINHOLD NIEBUHR** believed that all human history—whether your personal history, the history of your country, or the history of the world—is limited and incomplete. Meaning in life can only come from an eternal source. Therefore, we should have faith in God.

Nineteenth-century Japanese philosopher **KEIJI NISHITANI** believed human lives are meaningless. Some philosophers believe there is meaning in human life, while others have denied those meanings. In Nishitani's view, their views cancel one another out. We are left with a clear and true state of mind—absolute emptiness.

ALBERT CAMUS was a twentieth-century Algerian-French philosopher who felt the myth of Sisyphus shows how meaningless human life is. Each day you start with new hopes. For example, you plan to go to a movie that is supposed to be hilarious. At the end of the day, you can't help but feel disappointed. The movie wasn't that funny, and now you have to brush your teeth and get ready for bed again. The next day you start with new hopes. Maybe you are trying a new video game. Then you stop and notice the pattern. Nothing ever really satisfies you for very long. What should you do? Just give up? Camus says no. We must realize that pointlessness is a part of being human and we must accept it.

RICHARD TAYLOR was a twentieth-century American philosopher who came up with a new way to look at the myth of Sisyphus. Suppose the gods allow Sisyphus to carry a new rock up the hill each day so that he can build a magnificent temple at the top. Each day he adds one rock. All day, while he's carrying the rock, he thinks about where it will go and how the temple will look. But just when he completes the temple, it crumbles—without anyone seeing it. The next day, Sisyphus starts a new temple. Although the result is the same over and over, Sisyphus comes to enjoy his work. Would his enjoyment make Sisyphus's life meaningful? Taylor said, "Not exactly." Sisyphus's life would be meaningful because the design of the temple matters to him as an expression of his creativity.

Make a list of some activities you find meaningless. Make a list of some activities you find meaningful. Compare the lists to see why they are different. Does their meaningfulness depend on any of the following factors:

- Whether you enjoy it?
- Whether you get credit for it?
- Whether you have to do it repeatedly?
- Whether you chose to do it or someone else made you do it?
- Whether it is creative?

What do you think would make your life more meaningful?

Questions about Logic:

IF THIS IS TRUE, WHAT ELSE IS TRUE?

My dear reader, I am so proud to announce that I have decided to run for president! You should vote for me! Here's why:

Reason One:	Peace is good.
Reason Two:	Pollution is bad.
Reason Three:	I love dogs.
Conclusion:	You should vote for me!

What do you think? Convincing? Would you vote for me? Do you think this speech will get me elected?

No? But why not? Who could disagree with my reasons?

Oh, yeah—a good argument isn't just about good reasons. It's about good reasons that are *logically connected* to the conclusion. Looks like we are going to need to do some work on logic.

What is an ARGUMENT?

I n philosophy, an argument is a set of reasons that lead to a conclusion. The conclusion is the statement you're trying to prove. The reasons must provide logical, or reasonable, support for that conclusion. This makes an argument different from an explanation. Both may use the word "because," but they each use this word differently. Consider the following statements:

A. I'm running for president because I want to live in Washington, DC.

B. You should vote for me because I am better than the other candidates.

Statement A is an explanation. Statement B is an argument—or at least the beginning of an argument. It just needs more details about why I am better than the others.

One type of argument is a categorical **syllogism**. It is made of two statements, or reasons, and a conclusion. The statements connect to the conclusion by putting things in groups. For example:

1. No lizards are philosophers.
2. Leo is a lizard.

Therefore, Leo is not a philosopher.

Another type of argument is called *modus ponens*. Modus ponens starts with an "If . . . then" statement and then confirms that the "if" is true. For example:

1. If philosophy is important, then it should be taught at school.
2. Philosophy *is* important.

Therefore, philosophy should be taught at school.

Another type of argument is called *modus tollens*. Modus tollens starts with an "If . . . then" statement but then denies the "then" part. For example:

1. If Christopher Columbus really discovered America, then there wouldn't have been people here when he arrived.
2. There *were* people here when he arrived.

Therefore, Christopher Columbus did not really discover America.

Seventeenth-century philosopher **BLAISE PASCAL** used modus ponens to argue for belief in God. He didn't have evidence, so he decided there is a fifty-fifty chance that God exists. But being a gambler, he decided to bet on God. He figured he had nothing to lose and everything to gain by believing. His argument goes like this:

1. If it is possible that there is a being who will give an eternal reward to only those who believe in him, then we should believe in him.
2. It *is* possible that there is a being who will give an eternal reward to only those who believe in him.

Therefore, we should believe in him.

The Australian philosopher **J. L. MACKIE** used modus tollens to argue that God does not exist. Mackie noticed that the three major world religions—Christianity, Judaism, and Islam—agree that God is all-good, all-powerful, and all-knowing. If God was missing any of these qualities, he would not be the supreme being described in their holy books. Yet a god with these qualities wouldn't allow the unnecessary suffering we see in the world. Mackie's argument goes like this:

1. If an all-good, all-powerful, all-knowing God exists, then unnecessary suffering should not exist.
2. Unnecessary suffering *does* exist.

Therefore, an all-good, all-powerful, all-knowing God does not exist.

THINK ON IT!

1. Write a categorical syllogism proving that rocks are not animals because they are not alive.

2. Write a modus ponens argument proving that rabbits are mammals because they are warm-blooded.

3. Write a modus tollens argument proving that pigs can't fly because they do not have wings.

4. Write a categorical syllogism, modus ponens argument, or modus tollens argument proving a conclusion of your own.

What is the DIFFERENCE between a GOOD argument and a BAD one?

In a good argument, if the reasons are true, then the conclusion *has to* be true. In a categorical syllogism, you can test whether the reasons support the conclusion by drawing a diagram.

1. All As are in group B.

2. Group B is in group C.

3. Therefore, all As are in group C.

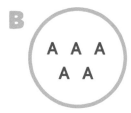

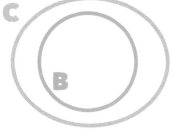

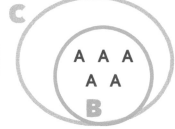

If you agree to the first and second steps, then you simply can't reject the conclusion. This is called "deduction." But there are many other types of syllogisms.

A *disjunctive syllogism* uses "or." For example:

1. Either the maid did it or the butler did it.
2. It wasn't the maid.

Therefore, it must have been the butler.

We call this type of reasoning "process of elimination." You can also consider more than two possibilities if you want.

A *hypothetical syllogism* concludes with an "if." For example:

1. If you love chocolate chip cookies, then you like chocolate.
2. If you like chocolate, then you'll eat beans.

Therefore, if you love chocolate chip cookies, then you'll eat beans.

You can have more than three steps, as long as each connects to the last.

A *statistical syllogism* lets you make an educated guess. For example:

1. Most kids like trampolines.
2. Jeremy is a kid.

Therefore, Jeremy probably likes trampolines.

Unlike other types of syllogisms we have looked at, this conclusion is not guaranteed.

ZENO OF CITIUM was an ancient Phoenician philosopher who loved to use syllogisms. While some philosophers have disorganized arguments, Zeno preferred to present his arguments in three clear steps. He would ask his opponents if they agreed to the first two steps—they usually did. Then he would show them how those two steps result in a surprising conclusion that they could not deny. Here are two examples:

1. Whatever uses reason is better than whatever does not use reason.
2. But nothing is better than the universe.

Therefore, the universe uses reason.

1. A god is worthy of honor.
2. Nonexistent things are not worthy of honor.

Therefore, a god exists.

Do you agree that the first two steps of each of these arguments are true? Do you agree that they result in the conclusions?

FRANCIS BACON was a seventeenth-century English philosopher who argued against the use of syllogisms to reason about the world. Instead, he preferred induction—the method of gathering evidence to support a general conclusion. For example:

1. Swan A is white.
2. Swan B is white.
3. Swan C is white.
4. And so on, for as many swans as we can find.

Therefore, probably, all swans are white.

Bacon argued against syllogistic reasoning as follows:

1. Syllogisms are made up of statements.
2. Statements are made up of words.
3. Words represent ideas.
4. Ideas are confused.

Therefore, syllogisms are confused.

The problem is that this argument is a syllogism. So, Bacon is using a syllogism against the use of syllogism!

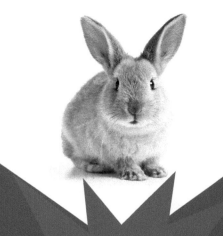

THINK ON IT!

Fix each of the following arguments to change them from a bad argument into a good argument.

Argument A

1. Either the philosopher, the biologist, or the poet did it.

2. The philosopher did not do it.

Therefore, the poet did it.

Argument B

1. All rabbits are furry.

2. Peter is a rabbit.

Therefore, Peter is fast.

Can an analogy prove ANYTHING?

rgument by **analogy** is a special type of **inductive reasoning** where you try to show that one thing is like another thing. Here is an example:

1. Cats are like humans in many ways.
2. Humans need love.

   Therefore, cats need love.

This is inductive reasoning because it begins with similarities we know about and tries to suggest another similarity based on them. But the conclusion is not guaranteed by the first two steps. It could be that, although cats are like human beings in many ways, love is one way in which they are different. There are three criteria, or standards, for judging an argument by analogy.

First, how relevant are the known similarities? We see that cats often play with their kittens just like human mothers play with their babies. This is relevant since play involves touching, just as love involves touching. Trees, in contrast, don't play or love, as far as we know. They can't touch one another on purpose.

Second, how strong are the similarities? Cats are aware of their surroundings, but are they self-aware the way humans are? They can't recognize themselves in the mirror. Gorillas, who can recognize themselves in the mirror, might be more similar to a human than a cat.

Third, how many similarities are there and how varied are they? Cats care for their young the way humans do. Cats are playful like humans. Cats are warm-blooded. How many more similarities can you think of? Are they within a limited range of qualities or do they span across a wide range?

Seventeenth-century theologian **WILLIAM PALEY** used an analogy to argue for the existence of God. Suppose you are hiking in the wilderness and find a watch on the ground. It couldn't be there randomly like the rest of the wilderness. Someone must have dropped it. Likewise, when we look at the universe, we see our blue-green world alone among bare, rocky planets. Earth can't be there randomly, like the rest of outer space. Someone must have put it there. We can summarize Paley's argument as follows:

1. A watch in the wilderness is like our world in the universe.
2. A watch was designed by a designer.

Therefore, our world was designed by a designer.

Nineteenth-century biologist **CHARLES DARWIN** used an analogy to argue for his theory of evolution. Suppose you are pigeon breeder who wants to produce a superstrong pigeon. How would you accomplish this? You would mate your strongest female pigeon with your strongest male pigeon. When they had babies, you would again mate the strongest female with the strongest male. You would do this over and over again. Each generation would become a little bit stronger. Over time, you would produce your super pigeon. Darwin hypothesized that nature works the same way:

1. Nature is like a pigeon breeder.
2. A pigeon breeder creates pigeons with new traits by mating animals with those traits.

Therefore, nature creates animals with new traits by mating animals with those traits.

THINK ON IT!

1. Write an argument by analogy that concludes playing a video game is good for you because it is like creating a work of art.

2. Write an argument by analogy that concludes video games are bad for you because playing them is like eating candy.

3. Write an argument by analogy that concludes playing video games is like eating because it matters what kind of game you play and how much you play.

4. Write your own argument by analogy about video games.

Is LOGIC the same as MATH?

Here's a test for you:

1. BIRD is to **NEST** just as _____ is to _____.

a) DOG : LEASH   c) BEAVER : DAM

b) SQUIRREL : NUT   d) CAT : LITTER BOX

2. 4 is to **2** just as _____ is to _____.

a) 3 : 7   c) 20 : 10

b) 7 : 3   d) 10 : 13

These are analogy problems. The answer to question one is (C), since the relationship between bird and nest is "the first builds the second." The answer to question two is (C), since the relationship between 4 and 2 is "the first doubles the second." The first question is logical, the second is mathematical—yet, they are both about relationships between things. Does this mean logic is the same as math?

Nineteenth-century German philosopher **GOTTLOB FREGE** argued that logic is the same as math. He believed that numbers exist in a place beyond the physical world. We use number symbols (2, 17, 100, for example) to represent numbers, but we can also use other symbols (x, y, z, for example) to represent things in the physical world. He developed a complex system for symbolizing **deductive arguments**.

Twentieth-century German mathematician **DAVID HILBERT** disagreed with Frege. In his view, math is like a game, not in the sense that you win or lose, but in the sense that the system is self-contained. When we play chess, the pieces are symbols of kings and queens, but they don't stand for any real people at all—the pieces only represent something inside the game. Likewise, when we use numbers, they do not represent anything existing in a place beyond the physical world.

Present-day American philosopher **SHARON BERRY** points out that whether logic is the same as math depends on what you mean. If by "logic" you mean general rules of reasoning, then logic is the same as math. Set theory—a type of math that uses circle diagrams—is the link between math and logic.

Eleventh-century Italian philosopher **ANSELM OF CANTERBURY** developed a proof for the existence of God. A proof is used in math to show that a mathematical idea is true. To prove: A triangle has three sides.

1. A triangle must have three angles.
2. Suppose a triangle does not have three sides.
3. Then we would have a triangle without three angles, which is impossible.

Therefore, a triangle must have three sides.

This is what Anselm's proof for God looks like: To prove: That God exists.

1. By definition, God is the greatest being
2. Suppose God does not exist.
3. Then we could imagine an existing god that is greater than the greatest being, which is impossible.

Therefore, God must exist.

Eleventh-century French philosopher **GAUNILO** disagreed with Anselm. He insisted that abstract reasoning can't prove the existence of anything. He wrote a parody, making fun of Anselm's argument. It went like this: To prove: That Blessed Island exists. Suppose the greatest conceivable island does not exist.

1. By definition, Blessed Island is the greatest island.
2. Suppose Blessed Island does not exist.
3. Then we could imagine an existing island that is greater than the greatest island, which is impossible.

Therefore, Blessed Island exists.

THINK ON IT!

1. Write a logical analogy.

2. Write a mathematical analogy.

3. The geometry-style proof we looked at is called "*reductio ad absurdum,*" which means "to shrink your opponent's view to an absurdity." When philosophers use the term "absurd" they don't mean "silly." They mean "impossible" or "contradictory." Write a *reductio ad absurdum* proof for the conclusion that your birthday only comes one day per year.

4. Write a *reductio ad absurdum* proof for a conclusion of your own.

Does the opinion of an AUTHORITY figure count as GOOD REASON?

Philosophers try to construct good arguments for their views and for critiquing the arguments of others. A good argument must get its conclusion from good reasons. Philosophers have noticed that humans naturally tend to use many bad reasons called **fallacies**. Let's look at some of the most common fallacies so that you can watch out for them.

An authority figure is someone with the knowledge and importance to be in charge—teachers, parents, and police officers are authorities. The fallacy called *ad verecundiam* (meaning "from reverence") is when you rely on an authority that is not relevant, or appropriate, for the argument. Take this statement, for example: "There is life on other planets—because my dad says so!" If you want to make an argument for life on other planets, you need evidence.

Consider an authority's **relevance**. For example, suppose you injured your knee and now you're trying to decide whether or not to join the ski club. Your doctor (a human health expert who has also examined your knee) has a relevant opinion.

Be careful. It's common for authorities to offer opinions that are not relevant to their knowledge. While your doctor may have a useful opinion about your knee's ability to handle ski club, her opinions about your friends, your clothes, the video games you play, or the books you read carry no special weight.

In the end, **any authority can be wrong**. Philosophers are doubtful of anyone who expects others to believe them without proof. Two favorite philosophical slogans throughout history have been *Nullius in verba*, meaning "take no one's word for it," and *Sapere aude*, meaning "dare to think for yourself!"

Nineteenth-century American philosopher and poet **RALPH WALDO EMERSON** wrote inspiring words against the *ad verecundiam* fallacy: "Nothing is at last sacred but the integrity of your own mind." By this he meant we should never let authorities pressure us into going against our own best judgment. For example, young people are taught to respect their elders. But respect is not the same as blind obedience. We each have a responsibility to be true to ourselves. We should resist any argument that doesn't give a good reason. "Because I said so" isn't a good reason. It may seem rude to point this out. But Emerson wrote that we should try to be brave enough to "speak the rude truth in all ways."

MARY WOLLSTONECRAFT was an eighteenth-century English philosopher and feminist. In her day, authorities wouldn't let women do many things men were allowed to do: vote in elections, hold political office, join the military, own property, get a divorce, play sports, or have their own bank accounts. Wollstonecraft argued that this discrimination against women was keeping society from being the best it could be. The only solution was to give boys and girls equal education so both had the opportunity to lead full lives. Education helps us develop independence of character which means we no longer bow to any authority except the authority of reason.

THINK ON IT!

Do you think the following arguments commit the *ad verecundiam* fallacy? Why or why not?

1. Xavier insists on staying up until midnight on New Year's Eve. His mother argues that he cannot function on so little sleep. She should know since she is his mother.

2. Audrey argues that the kids in her class should not challenge their teacher's decision to hold recess indoors today. The teacher has the right to decide.

3. Give your own *ad verecundiam* example.

Should I criticize PEOPLE or the IDEAS people have?

nother common fallacy to beware of is called *ad hominem*, meaning "against the person." This is a reasoning mistake you have probably seen many times. For example, Gina might say, "Mrs. Hertzfeldt is a terrible teacher. I mean, just look at her! She's wearing orange pants with a green sweater." Is clothing relevant to how well a person can teach? Probably not. I can imagine a great teacher in orange pants and a green sweater! Gina is attacking Mrs. Hertzfeldt personally instead of judging her teaching ability. Here are three more closely related fallacies:

Tu quoque, meaning you also, is when you try to disprove someone by claiming they do the very thing they are criticizing. Suppose Shadi is arguing that a local factory should be shut down because it is polluting the environment. Keri dismisses him, saying, "You pollute the environment too, Shadi—every time you throw away a Styrofoam cup."

Guilt by association is when you try to disprove your opponent by claiming they are connected to a bad group of people. For example, Keri might continue to attack Shadi by pointing out that the members of one environmentalist group have been spraying graffiti all around town.

Circumstantial *ad hominem* is when you try to disprove your opponent by claiming their argument stems from personal interest. For example, Keri might say, "The real reason Shadi wants the factory shut down is because he wants the land to be turned into a park where he and his friends can play basketball."

JEAN-JACQUES ROUSSEAU

was an eighteenth-century French philosopher who wrote a popular book called *Émile*, about how to raise children. In his day, children were strictly controlled and forced to learn all sorts of useless things. Rousseau presented an alternative—supporting freedom for students to learn from their own experiences. He argued that children are born good and wise in their own way. Rousseau had five children of his own, but didn't want to raise a family, so he sent them to an orphanage. Some people think that this shows his theories about children are worthless. Do you agree, or are they committing the *ad hominem* fallacy?

MARTIN HEIDEGGER was a twentieth-century German philosopher who wrote an important book called *Being and Time* about the meaning of existence. In this book, Heidegger argues that the highest moral authority comes from the free choices of true individuals. In 1933, Heidegger joined the Nazi party, which committed terrible crimes against millions of people. Even after he learned about those crimes, Heidegger never seemed to feel regret about them. Furthermore, he supported Nazi ideas in his journals. Some people insist that this shows his theories about morality are wrong. Do you agree, or are they committing the *ad hominem* fallacy?

THINK ON IT!

Do you think the following arguments commit the *ad hominem* fallacy? Why or why not?

1. Nya is deciding whether or not to join the soccer team. Joel argues that she shouldn't join because most of the girls on the team are mean.

2. Henry wants to sign up for an after-school art club, but sees all the names on the list are girls' names. A voice inside his head argues that he shouldn't sign up for an all-girl club.

3. 3. Give your own example of an *ad hominem* fallacy.

Is a POPULAR VIEW a true one?

I have more great news for you, my dear reader! A recent poll shows that 95 percent of voters are planning to vote for me for president. This proves I am the best candidate once and for all!

What? You're not so sure?

But why not? When all your friends bought that one thing-amajig, you decided you just had to buy one, too. You might have pleaded, "Please, Mom—everybody has one!" And when all your friends were doing that one thing, you decided you just had to do it, too. "Please, Mom—everybody's doing it!"

Actually, on the printed page, this reasoning looks pretty silly, doesn't it? That's because it's fallacious, or logically flawed.

The **bandwagon fallacy** (also called *ad populum*) is when you try to prove your conclusion by showing that it's already popular. For example, "Everyone wants a new puppy!" In the old days, a band wagon was a cart for the band in a circus parade. A party on wheels, it was designed to lure everyone in town to the circus.

The **snob appeal fallacy** is when you try to prove your conclusion by showing that an elite group of people already accept it. For example, "All the cool kids ride their bikes without helmets." Like the bandwagon fallacy, the snob appeal fallacy uses peer pressure to make people accept the argument.

Similar fallacies include the **appeal to pity** ("If you don't pick me for the team, I might start to cry.") and the **appeal to threat** ("Pick me for the team or I'll tell everyone you have a crush on Rowan."). Pity and threats don't count as good reasons for team-picking.

Nineteenth-century German philosopher **KARL MARX** was deeply concerned about poor people. He studied how business works to find out why the rich keep getting richer while others don't have any food to eat. He presented a vision of a different system, called communism, where everyone would be equal. People didn't like Marx's criticism of business. They arrested him and tried to prevent him from publishing his ideas. Only eleven people came to his funeral. But in the twentieth century, Marx's ideas became popular. Millions of copies of his books sold all around the world. Today, Marx is considered one of the most important writers of all time. Did his earlier unpopularity prove his ideas were wrong? Did his later popularity prove they were right?

LAOZI was an ancient Chinese philosopher who founded Daoism, a Chinese philosophy. *Dao* means "the way." The way of Daoism is the path of least resistance, or the easiest way to move forward. Picture a river flowing home to the sea. The goal is to let go of human confines like church and school in order to become one with nature. Laozi himself did this. He started out as a scholar in the royal court. People liked his ideas, but Laozi soon realized he didn't want to be famous. In fact, he thought popularity was a bad thing, so he wrote down his ideas and disappeared. His book recommends people live simple, humble lives. He wrote, "Knowing others is intelligence; knowing yourself is true wisdom."

THINK ON IT!

Do you think the following arguments commit the *ad populum* fallacy? Why or why not?

1. God must exist since millions of people all around the world believe in God.

2. No one likes a trash-talking kid. You better clean up your language.

3. Bichon dogs make great pets because everyone loves them.

4. This news must be important. It's trending on all the social media.

5. Let's see how this movie does at the box office before we buy tickets.

How do I
DEBATE
an issue?

Now that you've arrived at the end of this book, you've seen different philosophers' positions on big questions in metaphysics, epistemology, and ethics. You've also looked at the logical skills philosophers use to make arguments for their positions. You're now ready to develop your own philosophy, just like they did!

Remember that Socrates, the founder of philosophy, refused to write any books. He was firmly convinced that the search for wisdom must involve others in discussion. A debate is a discussion between two people who take opposite sides of an issue. Here are some final thoughts to guide your debates going forward.

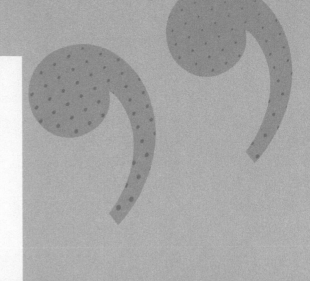

Define your terms. So often we think we disagree with someone when really we aren't even talking about the same thing! For example, I say my dog is a person. You say he isn't. But what I mean is that my dog has a point of view. What you mean is that he isn't human. Once we get clear on what we mean, we see that we're both right.

Be considerate. When you really do disagree with someone, you may find yourself not wanting to listen to them. But do listen—find out what they are trying to say. You may actually need to help them explain what they mean. Interpret their words in the best possible light and show that you understand their perspective. Hopefully, they will return the favor!

Support your view. It's not enough to just have an opinion. And you shouldn't just criticize your opponent. You need to have reasons and evidence for your view. Why do you believe what you do? You may find that you're not sure. Do some thinking. Do some research. In the process, you may find yourself changing your mind. This is a sign of growth.

JOHN DEWEY was a twentieth-century American philosopher who argued that debate is a necessary part of life in a democratic society. Democracy means government by the people. In order to govern themselves, people need to be informed about current issues and able to discuss them in a respectful way. Dewey also believed that education is not preparation for life, but rather life itself. This suggests that kids who live in a democratic society need to debate issues—not just as practice for when they grow up, but as a way of participating in their society. The most important part of democracy comes before any vote—thinking about and discussing both sides of the issues.

Twentieth-century English philosopher **BERTRAND RUSSELL** warns us that sometimes debating may make us less certain of our views. He also instructs us not to worry about that. Uncertainty is a good thing. The main job of philosophy is to free us from certainties that close our minds. A philosopher may find out that many issues, when explored, lead to problems and incomplete answers. This is okay! When you have the courage to explore your doubt, you can come closer to the truth. The worst mistake is to look for facts and statements that match what you already believe. This is called "cherry picking." Instead, expand your mind with the amazing things you encounter on your search. Russell writes, "Through the infinity of the universe, the mind which contemplates it achieves some share in infinity."

THINK ON IT!

Gather some friends together and hold a debate. First, pick an issue, such as whether or not eating meat is wrong. Then pick a side. It doesn't matter if you haven't completely made up your mind yet. In fact, you may want to try taking a side at random, just to see what it's like. Build your argument with reasons you can back up with evidence. Anticipate the objections your opponents might have and try to answer them. Remember that, for philosophers, the goal is not to win the debate, but rather to come a little closer to finding the truth.

GLOSSARY

analogy: A comparison or similarity between two things

anarchist: Someone who believes there should be no government

coherentist: Someone who believes knowledge is justified when beliefs fit together

compatibilist: Someone who believes we can be free even if our actions are determined

debate: A discussion of an issue where people give arguments for opposing viewpoints

deductive argument: When the steps of an argument make the conclusion necessary

democracy: Government by the people

determinist: Someone who believes all our actions are caused by past events or laws of nature

empiricist: Someone who believes knowledge comes from experience through the five senses

epistemology: The study of knowledge

eternal: Something without beginning or end

ethics: The study of moral value

faith: Belief without evidence

fallacy: A mistake in reasoning

feminist: Someone who believes in equal rights for women

foundationalist: Someone who believes knowledge must be built from basic certainties

free will: Having the power to act for or against our desires

inductive reasoning: When the steps of an argument make the conclusion probable or likely

justified/justification: Having the right to make a claim

libertarian: Someone who believes that human beings have free will

logic: The study of good reasoning

metaphysics: The study of reality

moral/morality: Concerned with right and wrong behavior

pacifist: Someone who is against war and violence

paradigm: A mental pattern or model

paradox: A statement that seems impossible at first but turns out to be true

reality: The way things are

skepticism/skeptical: Doubting the truth of what someone says

soul: The spiritual part of a person

stoicism: Living life without showing emotions

syllogism: A short argument showing steps leading to a conclusion

theologian: A person who studies God

theory: A set of linked ideas to explain something

thought experiment: An imaginary scenario designed to test a theory

universal: The same for everyone, everywhere

virtue theorist (epistemology): Someone who believes knowledge comes from being a person with a good attitude

virtue theorist (ethics): Someone who believes morality comes from being a person with good habits

RESOURCES

Big Ideas for Curious Minds: An Introduction to Philosophy, by Anna Doherty

    This book is an introduction to the history of philosophy and its concepts.

Children's Book of Philosophy: An Introduction to the World's Great Thinkers and Their Big Ideas, published by DK Children

    This brightly illustrated book introduces kids to central concepts in philosophy.

The Cartoon Introduction to Philosophy, by Michael F. Patton and Kevin Cannon

    This humorous, comic-book-style book introduces the history of philosophy.

Philosophy for Kids: 40 Fun Questions That Help You Wonder about Everything!, by David White

    This is a textbook introduction to central questions in philosophy.

INDEX

ACKNOWLEDGMENTS

I would like to thank John Carroll University for supporting my work on this volume.

ABOUT THE AUTHOR

SHARON KAYE is a professor of philosophy at John Carroll University in Cleveland, Ohio. She graduated Phi Beta Kappa from the University of Wisconsin–Madison in 1992 and received her PhD from the University of Toronto in 1997. She publishes articles, textbooks, and philosophical novels while directing a Philosophy for Kids program.

CPSIA information can be obtained
at www.ICGtesting.com
Printed in the USA
BVHW052133181120
593430BV00001B/1

9 781647 391034